Peacock Blue

THE COLLECTED POEMS OF PHYLLIS WEBB

EDITED BY JOHN F. HULCOOP

Talonbooks

Talonbooks
278 East First Avenue, Vancouver, British Columbia, Canada v5t 1a6
www.talonbooks.com

First printing: 2014

Typeset in Arno
Printed and bound in South Korea

Interior and cover design by Typesmith
Cover illustration: Detail from Phyllis Webb's *Peacock Blue*, acrylic and
collage on canvas, photographed by Janet Dwyer
Cover photograph of Phyllis Webb by Diana Hayes, www.dianahayes.ca

Talonbooks gratefully acknowledges the financial support of the Canada
Council for the Arts, the Government of Canada through the Canada
Book Fund, and the Province of British Columbia through the British
Columbia Arts Council and the Book Publishing Tax Credit.

Library and Archives Canada Cataloguing in Publication
Webb, Phyllis, 1927–
[Collected poems]
    Peacock blue : the collected poems / Phyllis Webb ;
edited by John F. Hulcoop.

isbn 978-0-88922-912-9 (bound).—isbn 978-0-88922-914-3 (pbk.)

    I. Hulcoop, John F., 1930–, editor II. Title.

ps8545.e22a17 2014   c811'.54   c2014-902686-2

and I shall be single
minded and absolute
easy not easy
not ease
I would call my
pleasure home
but is a far
outpost and pleasing
not pleasing
harder to get at
when said
said
of the lustre

Contents

Trio (1954)

Even Your Right Eye (1956)

I.

The Sea Is Also a Garden (1962)

Naked Poems (1965)

Wilson's Bowl (1980)

Water and Light: Ghazals and Anti Ghazals (1984)

Hanging Fire (1990)

Uncollected and Unpublished Poems

Introduction

> but I tell you,
> *Fishstar,* the colour of chaos was not
>
> Peacock blue.
> – "The Birds," *Water and Light*

"I don't want to say anything. I have no message for the world." This wayward start to a 2002 interview with Jay Ruzesky is not uncharacteristic of Phyllis Webb, who has a playful, often disruptive sense of humour. In a 1993 interview with Janice Williamson, Webb – the experienced broadcaster – responded to what sounds like a peroration praising the poet's "brave" writing and her "struggle with the sharp edges of life" with "complex 'last things'" and "difficult 'finalities'," by remarking wryly, "You're not on air, you know, just tape." In *Trio,* her very first collection of published poems, we encounter the devilish Webb at work:

> I like this high-tailing it to hell
> and almost swell it is to kick up
> blue dust atmospheric
> (especially when one is used to
> regulated black or white dust cleric).
> – "Earth Descending"

Of course, Webb found many things to say to Jay Ruzesky and, in a slightly oblique manner, she did deliver her message to the world, the same message poets have been delivering ever since we began chanting, singing, making songs, and telling stories:

> There's all that pleasure. "The pleasure of the text" –
> Roland Barthes's phrase. For me, there's a lot of pleasure
> in writing ... and [I] want to give pleasure as well by
> producing something splendid ... (254)

She admits to being aware of an audience somewhere at the back of her mind and thinks that "someone might want to look at this [poem or book]," might "happen to look at it and then see something" and realize that she is "the maker of possibly beautiful things." Wordsworth, an acknowledged presence in Webb's earliest work, declared that the poet "writes under one constriction only, namely that of ... giving pleasure." And Wallace Stevens, another numinous presence in Webb's world, is certain that the "purpose of poetry is to contribute to man's happiness."

Peacock Blue: The Collected Poems is in itself "something splendid." It will certainly contribute to the happiness of readers by giving them pleasure; it will also suggest that, despite Webb's sense of herself as "minimalist producer" (*NBBS*, 136), she has a lot to say about the pain as well as the pleasures of existence, about the relationship between being and nothingness, life and death. This collection contains more than three hundred poems; it not only sets the keystone on her long and distinguished creative career, but also contains all kinds of "messages" for the world, including an enigmatic cat poem (one of several) actually entitled "Messages." *Peacock Blue* gathers together the poems that constitute her eight previously published volumes: *Trio: First Poems by Gael Turnbull, Phyllis Webb, and E.W. Mandel* (1954); *Even Your Right Eye* (1956); *The Sea Is Also a Garden* (1962); *Naked Poems* (1965); *Wilson's Bowl* (1980); *Sunday Water: Thirteen Anti Ghazals* (1982); *Water and Light* (1984); and *Hanging Fire* (1990). It contains, in addition, two poems first published in *Selected Poems, 1954–1965* (1971), and two that first appeared in *The Vision Tree: Selected Poems by Phyllis Webb* (1982). More importantly and most excitingly for those who know and love Webb's work, *Peacock Blue* contains nearly fifty poems previously uncollected, some of which have never before been seen in print.

The introduction to a volume of this kind is neither a biography, though some biographical details will inevitably emerge; nor is it a critical appraisal, though the fact that I've been reading and writing about Webb's work since 1965, and happily agreed to edit the *Collected Poems,* betrays in advance my own critical position. Like a large number of writers, creative and critical, I regard Phyllis Webb as one of Canada's finest poets, sometimes difficult and often challenging, but always thoughtful, always rewarding to poetry readers seeking pleasure. Douglas Barbour pronounced Webb's *Naked Poems* "one of the most influential works of its time, for it suggested a new vision of the book-length poem which profoundly affected a number of poets in the following literary generations." Tom Marshall, writing on the major Canadian poets in *Harsh and Lovely Land,* was moved to call *Naked Poems* "perhaps the most beautiful love poems to have been written in Canada" (117–18). Northrop Frye saw *Wilson's Bowl* as "a landmark in Canadian poetry." And Webb's two succeeding volumes, as well as some of the late, uncollected poems like "The Tree Speaks," prove Webb to be, in W.J. Keith's words, "the consummate poet, with a wonderfully controlled tone, a sense of wry fantasy, and a gift for the colloquial" – much in evidence in her best poetry. George Woodcock settles, once and for all, the matter of Webb's reputation as a poet. He claims that "the clarity of her vision and the dedicated impeccability of her craft" entitle her "to a first place not merely among recent Canadian poets but in the whole poetic tradition of our land" (265).

PHYLLIS WEBB, PRIVATE AND PUBLIC

> "It's unfortunate that we have lives. The work doesn't need that dimension."
>
> – Webb in interview with Jay Ruzesky

In a 1993 lecture on "Poetry and Psychobiography" Webb asked "whether we should freight a work of art with extra-textual meaning and emotion." She never actually got around to answering the question; but, from statements she's made in several interviews, we know what her answer would be: No, we should not! "The body of work is not me ... I'm such a private person and I've gone to extremes to remain private, apart from my public performances" (Ruzesky, 226). She complicated her answer – and the question – by adding, "We [writers] don't want to be conned ... the work of the imagination can float free of all that biographical data. It never really floats free of the self" (227).

Without wanting to freight her poems with extra-textual meanings and emotions, however, a few biographical facts may prove useful to Webb's first-time readers. The youngest child and only daughter of Mary and Alfred Webb, Phyllis Jean was born in April 1927, the year that Proust published the final volume of *À la recherche* and Woolf, *To the Lighthouse.* She is a true child of Modernism as much of her early work proves. "I grew up on an island – Vancouver Island. I was born in Victoria ... and my one ambition as a teenager was to get off the island ... And then by half way through my life my ambition was to get back on an island" (Munton, 6–7). Though she's lived in Victoria, Vancouver, Edmonton, Toronto, and Montreal, as well as London, Paris, and San Francisco, Canada's West Coast, like a lodestone, has always pulled her home. Salt Spring Island has been her chosen residence more or less continuously for forty plus years: "I feel safe on this island. I feel protected from people" (10). Her vulnerability is not only a primary aspect of character, it's also been essential to her creative life: she is, as artists must be, peculiarly vulnerable to experience. Vulnerability comes at a price, however. Her parents divorced in the mid-1930s. Discussing *Hanging Fire,* her "most angry book," Webb says it seeks to widen the subject matter, to open up the domestic material where "a lot of the violence occurs." The violence, she adds, "has not been in my adult life so much as in my childhood" (*SK,* 32).

While attending a private school in Victoria ("I don't think I would have made it at a regular school" [Wachtel, 8]), Webb's social studies teacher took her class to visit the B.C. legislature. The Opposition leader, a member of the Co-operative Commonwealth Federation (CCF), was making his reply to the budget speech. It had "quite a dramatic impact on me," she remembered in an interview with Janice Williamson; such an impact "that I became involved with the CCF at that time. I began to learn about socialism" (323). Only twelve when the Second World War broke out, Webb has said it –

> was one of *the* formative experiences of my youth. It all came mainly through radio broadcasts and talk among people; also, my oldest brother, Walter, was in the war – he joined up at seventeen, and was overseas. But the horror and insanity of war, and of politics, turned me to socialism in my seventeenth year. (Letter, October 10, 1970)

At twenty-two, she would become the youngest person in the Commonwealth ever to run as an election candidate (for the CCF) (Wachtel, 11).

Webb took her undergraduate degree in English and philosophy at the University of British Columbia (UBC). Critics who object to the gnarled intellectuality of some of her work and her early probing of the dark side of life often forget about her training in philosophy. "I've always been a very questioning person ... ever since I was a child" (Munton, 6). "I have always had to seek a meaning. I was not handed it at birth ... I had never thought of phil. (phyl) as the study of death when I was studying it; but of course the search for meaning, for grounding, is made necessary by death. When my eye took in the Socratic question – 'For is not philosophy / the study of death?' it was as if my whole past interest in phil. was lit up" (Letter, July 31, 1986; see also "Socrates," *WB*).

At UBC, Webb's vocation as poet was encouraged by working with Roy Daniells (who taught Milton and the Metaphysical Poets), Earle Birney (who ran a writers' club off-campus), and John Creighton who taught an Introduction to Literature course that included on its reading list a good number of Canadian poets: P.K. Page was "the one who made me feel I wanted to be a poet" (Sujir). In fact, Webb had started writing poems while still at school (at least one, entitled "Ego," survives in the LAC fonds); "Introspective Lovers," later published in *Trio*, was written while she was still at university:

> When I was younger my intellectual concerns seemed to have something to do with the man that I was involved with and even my professors at UBC had a big influence on me. I was very susceptible to male influence, and I think that was because I lost my father at an early age through divorce. (Butling, 129)

The most powerful of all these influential males was F.R. Scott, whom Webb met and fell in love with – while attending the 1949 CCF National Convention in Vancouver (Scott was a founding member of the party). He "influenced my life enormously. He was a socialist when I was, he had a broad knowledge – a Renaissance man they used to call him" (Wachtel, 11). It was Scott who persuaded Webb to move to Montreal, where she met, mixed with, and befriended some of the leading poets of the time.

Scott introduced her into the literary circles that revolved around both *Preview* and *New Statement*, where she encountered Avi Boxer, Leonard Cohen, Louis Dudek, Irving Layton, Eli Mandel, A.J.M. Smith, John Sutherland, Gael Turnbull, and Miriam Waddington. Later, in Toronto, she "occasionally saw Ray Souster, and Al Purdy, and Earle Birney, Victor Coleman, Michael Ondaatje … In my work I ran into a lot of writers" (Ruzesky, 237). From 1950 to 1957, Webb worked as a secretary in Montreal and London; she also began doing freelance work for the Canadian Broadcasting Corporation (CBC) where, over the years, she interviewed poets and wrote dozens of book reviews of their works. In the summer of 1963 she covered the important poetry conference organized by Warren Tallman at UBC, interviewing Margaret Avison, Robert Creeley, Robert Duncan, Allen Ginsberg, Denise Levertov, and Charles Olson. Between April and July 1967, by which time she was executive producer of *Ideas* – the radio program she co-created with William Young and which, nearly fifty years later, is still aired every weeknight – she produced and hosted thirteen TV programs on poetry for which she interviewed at least thirty poets. She has always been very much a part of the community of Canadian poets, and is still pleased when she receives new publications from its younger members who admire her work and want her opinion of theirs.

Her first trip abroad (1954–55) was to Britain where, significantly, she made straight for Ireland to pay homage to Yeats and Joyce. Her second, supported by a Canadian Government Overseas Award in 1957, was to Paris, where she lived for eighteen months (1957–59). Here, it was not so much the poetry but the avant-garde French theatre, existential and absurd, that grabbed her attention: Sartre, Pirandello, Arthur Adamov, and Antonin Artaud (the Theatre of Cruelty). Artaud compared theatre with the plague, regarding it as a sort of "psychic entity" rather than a disease. "The plague takes dormant images, latent anarchy, pushing them abruptly into extreme gestures; the theatre too pushes gestures to their extreme." Our theatre, Artaud lamented, "has broken with the spirit of profound anarchy which is at the basis of all poetry" (Hayman, 90–91, 79). Writing in "Phyllis Webb's Canada," published in the October 1971 issue of *Maclean's*, the ironic Miss Webb archly remarked, "I am a voter who has never voted for a winning party, and a law-abiding anarchist. No party would have me if they knew what I was really thinking" (*T*, 12). A Canada Council Junior Arts Grant enabled

Webb to live almost a year (1963–64) in San Francisco, where from time to time she met with Robert Duncan. He became another of her powerful male mentors, valued especially for his sensitivity to the music of poetry.

By this time she had three books in print, was working on *Naked Poems* (1965), and thinking about a work of much greater proportions which would, perhaps, centre on the Russian anarchist-geographer Prince Kropotkin. "Too grand and too designed (the 'body politic' and 'love's body' as interchangeable polymorphous analogues in an ideal world)" (*WB*, 9), this work was never completed. What began as a study of power becomes, finally, a poem about different kinds of failure. Several sections "from *The Kropotkin Poems*" appear in *Wilson's Bowl* (1980). The Canada Council Senior Arts Grant awarded Webb in 1969 enabled her to quit her full-time job at the CBC and return to the West Coast, living mostly on Salt Spring Island. She continued to do freelance work for the CBC and taught creative writing at UBC (1976–77) and the University of Victoria, off and on (1978–1990). She was also writer-in-residence at the University of Alberta in Edmonton (1980–81). *The Vision Tree,* Webb's second *Selected Poems,* earned her the Governor General's Award for Poetry in 1982 – and the community of Canadian poets said, "About time too!" In the same year, she published *Sunday Water: Thirteen Anti Ghazals,* which shortly became the first section of *Water and Light: Ghazals and Anti Ghazals.* Different writers' conferences lured her abroad again: in 1989 to Finland, in 1991 to Germany, and in 1992 to Australia and New Zealand. *Hanging Fire,* her final volume of poetry, came out in 1990. She was honoured by being appointed an Officer of the Order of Canada in 1992. In 2001, with Catherine Hobbs, the archivist of literary manuscripts at the National Library, I co-curated *Phyllis Webb: Elemental,* an exhibition of her archival material. She is only the third woman to have been so distinguished: Susanna Moodie and Gabrielle Roy preceded her.

"There'll probably never be another book," she confided to Jay Ruzesky in 2002, adding "Well, you never know!" (252). That was the year I wrote an article about Webb for *Trek* magazine. In it I called co-curating the exhibition in Ottawa one of the highlights of my academic career. I added, "editing Webb's *Collected Poems* would be its keystone and complete a lifetime's work" (16). I urged Webb to allow a *Collected Poems* that year, but she refused. Little did we know that twelve years on there would indeed be "another book" and that I would be editing it.

Associating the end of her writing life with her mother's death, at which time she turned from poetry to painting, Webb told Ruzesky "it was not so much about stopping writing as withdrawing from being a 'poet'." After her trips abroad in 1992, she decided "'No more public appearances,' and I've pretty much stuck to that except for memorial occasions or ecological ones. And that led to an examination of the problem of the ego and identity. I wanted to see if I existed apart from my identity as a poet. That was an important part of who I thought I was" (232–33). The division appears almost unnaturally clear-cut here: Webb, the poet and public performer; Webb the woman, "always the good daughter" (*SK*, 34), the caring friend and undercover lover who has used all kinds of evasive strategies to keep her self to herself, who has spoken and even written a poem (unpublished) about her "Self-Willed Exile," and who has consequently been called "reclusive." In the foreword to *Talking*, her first prose collection (1982), Webb reflected, "I have always thought of myself as a quiet person, not much of a talker, perhaps the remnants of my shyness as a child, but when I was putting these radio talks and essays together I realized how much talking I have done in my life" (7).

"Social good has always been something I've cared about," Webb told Jay Ruzesky. He replied by asking if poems could ever serve "a social function" and about Webb's political involvement:

> My time with *Ideas* at CBC, my work generally at CBC, was very important and that was certainly political. We were a radical bunch and a lot of our programs dealt with very, very important social issues. That's probably when I was most effective in a public way. Teaching, too. That's also socially useful. (231–32)

"The Forgotten Freedom" (1957) is one example of such a program. The freedom discussed is freedom from noise. "The personal privacy of those who would elect silence is totally ignored and such people suffer a continual sense of auditory rape" (LAC). Protection of this forgotten freedom, she exclaimed, is really "a question of civil rights!" The talk seems more radical and even more relevant today than when it was written. In 1970 Webb launched a formal protest against CBC Vancouver's sexist hiring policies. When the corporation refused to consider her as a summer relief announcer, she wrote angrily against "the idea that the authority of the news must be endowed with a male voice." The B.C. Civil Liberties Association investigated the case – and won. The judgment against CBC Vancouver led to a radical change in its hiring policy (LAC). The next year Webb applied to join the activist crew of an old fishing boat called *The Greenpeace*, hoping to participate in the protest against America's underground nuclear test on the island of Amchitka. "Madly busy with Amnesty International (it's Prisoners of Conscience week)" – so she wrote to Daphne Marlatt in 1982, revealing another aspect of her social activism; "my life seems to be about to be taken over by AI" (*Festschrift*, 89). On Thanksgiving Day 1993, she stood on the steps of the B.C. Legislature and read her poem "The Tree Speaks," a protest against the government's continuing to allow logging in Clayoquot Sound. A public woman, indeed, though a very private person.

Forty-three years before "The Tree Speaks," Webb wrote the lines: "There has been a forest murdered, green promise broken." They appear in an unpublished poem, "Statement for History" (LAC), in which she also writes of "loggers at loggerheads / over possession ..." She alluded to this poem when asked if her politics and writing ever intersected:

> They didn't at the time. I did try to write about social subjects, like logging in B.C., and those few poems turned out really to be not very good poems ... once I got into the area of ideology, the poetry went bad ... If there is political content now, it comes in on its own and doesn't have to disrupt the poem. But it seemed to me I was going against that [lyrical] impulse and trying to shape the poem to the statement ... (Williamson, 324)

Asked about her feminism in the same interview, Webb observed, "I am seen increasingly as a feminist writer." But, she warns, "I refuse to identify myself ... I don't want to constrict myself with labels ... I began thinking about myself as a socialist, a left-wing person, not necessarily a writer, and that was a major identity for me for a long time. And then that shifted to anarchism, and then to feminism" (337). Pauline Butling has written a book on Webb's feminism, *Seeing in the Dark* (1997); many other women have written articles on the same subject. Only one critic, so far, has written on Webb's politics, especially her own brand of anarchism: Stephen Collis, *Phyllis Webb and the Common Good: Poetry / Anarchy / Abstraction* (2007).

THE LYRIC VOICE

> "What does it matter who's speaking, someone said, what does it matter?"
>
> – Samuel Beckett,
> *The Complete Short Prose, 1929–89*

Labelling Webb with very bold labels, both Collis and Butling tend to be reductive, though Collis's approach is a good deal more inclusive than Butling's. Both critics refer to "the death of the lyric," a subject Webb herself discusses at some length with Smaro Kamboureli. The middle section of *Hanging Fire* is, "among other things, about the death of the lyric poem and my sense that that comes out of the world we live in. We are not in Wordsworth land any more." Webb feels that "in the face of our social conditions ... the lyric response is almost impossible" (33-34). Such a statement inevitably calls to mind Adorno's opinion, "To write poetry after Auschwitz is barbaric. And this corrodes even the knowledge of why it has become impossible to write poetry today" (34) – lyric or otherwise. Despite which view, Phyllis Webb, like countless other poets, went right on writing poetry. The Holocaust, the many wars and revolutions fought since 1946, the current clashes in the Middle East and Middle Africa, the ecological disasters and contemporary economic crises have not, cannot in fact destroy or even obscure what Helen Vendler calls "the interior world of perception, emotion, and intellectual construction [which] has always seemed, to lyric poets, the locus of reality" (5). The older generation of lyricists (disillusioned, perhaps, by age and experience) will inevitably be succeeded by a younger, more energetic and hopeful generation – as Keats well knew when referring to "the eternal law" in *Hyperion*. The contemporary lyric poet's music is bound, for obvious reasons – historical, socio-economic, psychological – to sound less like Grieg's *Lyric Suite* than the *Lyric Suite* by Alban Berg, or the lyrical *Verwandlungsmusik* in Act One of his fiercely discordant opera *Lulu*. One of the great ironies of Webb's allusion in "To the Finland Station" to Barry McKinnon's *The Death of a Lyric Poet,* is the fact that it's followed by one of her loveliest lyrical poems, musically entitled "'Passacaglia'":

> The poet dives off the deep end
> of the lyric poem to surface on
> Nevsky Prospekt in Leningrad
> on a hot June night
> missing her friends who ought
> to be here in the hot night
> walking up Nevsky Prospekt
> she has broken her habit of
> repetition, the snowdrops,
> the snowdrops, the snowdrops
> in the white nights, white
> nights, white nights, the
> death of the lyric poem
> the death –

Significantly, the poem is not predicated on a lyric "I" but upon a third-person "poet" who is missing *her* friends – Timothy Findley and Bill Whitehead. In the preface to *Nothing But Brush Strokes,* her last published volume, Webb refers to "a multiple personality running loose in this book"; and in "Performance," a poem seized upon and much discussed by her critics, the speaker asks, "Who is this *I* infesting my poems? ... // I am the mask, the voice, the one who begins those lyrical poems, *I wandered lonely as a cloud ... / I hear the Shadowy Horses, their long manes a-shake ...*" And in that instant she confirms what every reader and writer of lyric poetry knows: the voice we hear in Webb as in Keats or Leonard Cohen –

> was heard
> In ancient days by emperor and clown:
> Perhaps the self-same song that found a path
> Through the sad heart of Ruth, when, sick for home,
> She stood in tears amid the alien corn;
> The same that oft-time hath
> Charm'd magic casements, opening on the foam
> Of perilous seas, in faery lands forlorn.

It belongs, here, to a nightingale, the poet's persona or mask through which sounds the ancient, universal, many-folded lyric voice. Indeed, it has been around for a very long time and probably predates literacy. We hear it singing even in the great epics from *Gilgamesh* on: Priam's plea to Achilles at the end of the *Iliad,* Dido's lament before dying in Book IV of the *Aeneid.* Possibly the first individual in Western history to use it is a woman, Sappho, whose texts, fragmented by time rather than the advent of Modernism, almost certainly played as big a part in shaping Webb's *Naked Poems* as did the haiku. Perhaps the most self-evident thing to say about the lyric "I" is that the universal use of the first-person singular pluralizes what it speaks to – *us. We* all identify with it because everything *we* say is predicated upon it. It is gender unmarked (unless the reader naively assumes that the poet's gender determines that of the voice). For example, these lines by the great Greek poet herself:

> The moon has set
> and the Pleiades, it's
> midnight, time goes by,
> I lie alone.

The speaker could just as well be a man as a woman. Brief as a naked poem, this lyric "I" is like Webb's famous "half-moon sketched in air," only half of the whole truth. Ostensibly calm and collected enough to write the poem, the speaking "I" implies a "hidden wholeness" that encompasses the pain of a lonely, maybe abandoned lover waiting, as it were, for the phone to ring – a situation *we* can all identify with. Here's Sappho's descendant, Webb:

> *Tonight*
> *quietness*
> *in the room.*
>
> *We knew*

Again, *we* the readers so identify with the speaker of this *Naked Poem* ("Suite II") that it doesn't matter what we are – lesbians, gay guys, straight men or women, African, Asian, or Caucasian – we don't need to be told what the speaker and her lover know. We know it too.

"*Listen*," commands the speaker in "Performance":

> Do you hear the *I* running away? … Look again. *I* is off and diving into Fulford Harbour to run with the whales. *I* spout. *I* make whalesong. Passengers on the ferry swarm to starboard to see me disporting myself. *I / we* know they are out to get us … *I* commits suicide in the watery commune, the vocal pod. *We* swims on.

Asked to perform at an Amnesty International event in Victoria, Webb needed something new to read (as she explains to Kamboureli): "So 'the performing whales' also get into it, and Amnesty being concerned with prisoners, I was concerned with whales as well. Actually, it's almost a conceit. I was writing a poem about performing the poem I was writing. The whole connection with the audience was definitely the main concern – apart from working out the role of the first-person singular" (37). And Webb certainly does give the first-person singular a good workout, transforming "I" into the non-gendered third-person singular ("*I* is off"), into the first-person plural ("we"), and into the objective and reflexive pronouns ("me," "us," "myself"). Webb's "conceit," her fanciful and elaborate metaphor for the poet-auditor relationship, is not only a *bravura* "performance" but also a playful warning to the reader (audience) *not* to take the plurivocal lyric "I" at *Fach* value. It may "commit suicide" but we / they swim on. "I" disappears in "the watery commune, the vocal pod." The first-person singular singer becomes a choir of many voices, many *I*'s, singing in many keys and many parts. "'We are not single, we are one'": this revelation occurs to Bernard the writer in Woolf's great lyrical novel, *The Waves*. In a transformative moment, plural is singularized, singular pluralized.

We do not, cannot naively identify the lyric "I" with the historically / geographically defined poet: "Here we are all, by day; by night, we're hurled / By dreams, each one into a several world." What does it matter who says this? The lyric voice utters a truth. We are moved by the words as arranged on the page or as spoken in the mouth. We don't need to know who writes or speaks. When Webb says at the start of an early poem, "I am promised / I have taken the veil" ("Poet," *Trio*), we do not mistake the poet for a nun, though the poet, dressed in a playful habit, may well be expressing the fear and anxiety she feels in committing herself (like a novice) to a vocation and to a community dominated by men: the community of poets in 1950s

Montreal. More difficult to distinguish from the author is the "I" at the end of "Poems of Failure" in *Wilson's Bowl*:

> I live
> alone. I have a phone. I shall go to Russia. One
> more day run round and the "good masterpiece of work"
> does not come. I scribble.

Momentarily, Webb the private woman, seems to have commandeered the speaking "I"; but when, in the next sentence, the "I" approaches "some distant dream" we know it's the poet who's in charge here. The "I" who speaks in "I Daniel" uses a more distinctly identified mask than the "I" in "Poet." When he laments, "the poetry tangled, no vision of my own to speak of," we may be tempted to confuse *her* with *him*, private person with *persona;* but the biblical Daniel separates not only his self from the poet's, but also his private from his public and prophetic self. Speaking of "Ambrosia" (in *Hanging Fire*), Webb confesses that the poem "has a disruptive 'I,' the 'I' of the unbeliever who is actually caught up in this ambrosial moment of writing the poem about Hopkins": "'I am so happy, so happy'." These words, says Webb the unbeliever, "were Hopkins' last words. These *words* become mine. And yet *I'm* still very separate from *him* (italics added). At the end of "Performance" the poet states, "I am only a partial fiction." Kamboureli wonders what Webb has in mind "with respect to the 'I' speaking and the act of constructing a fiction." The public woman replies: "I don't know how that it's possible to be anything but at least partly fictional when you're writing. *It is not life, it is writing.* So there is no way this *I* can be totally *me.* It's an artifact, a fiction …" (italics added). Kamboureli presses Webb. "To some extent, then, you're almost addressing the fundamental mystery of otherness … but you also demystify this otherness by presenting a much more direct, more easily accessible self." "It sounds lovely," says the wicked Webb, almost but not quite ending this charming conversation (37).

"Is Verse a Dying Technique?" Edmund Wilson asked in 1934. "Who Killed Poetry?" Joseph Epstein inquired in 1988. "Can Poetry Matter?" Dana Gioia pondered in 1991. In 1968, Barthes announced "The Death of the Author," and was echoed by Foucault and other deconstructionist critics. The "cardinal principle" of American language poets, according to Marjorie Perloff, "has been the dismissal of 'voice' as the foundational principle of lyric poetry." Ironically, absurdly, the non-existent "voices" of many of these "authors" can still be heard reading their poems in various venues, including the Internet. Like "the beat" in the lyrics of the famous Sonny and Cher song, the *voice* goes on. In the United States alone, Dana Gioia estimates, just under a thousand new books of poetry are published every year. In 2008, William Sieghart, founder of the Forward Prizes for Poetry in Britain, remarked on the "phenomenal growth of interest in poetry of all kinds since 1992," an observation updated by Tim Love in 2010. As for the so-called revolution, the anarchism of the language poets, Ron Silliman, a foremost exponent, confesses that "the revolution of the word is not an anarchist event. On the contrary, as the author" – not dead at all but still very much alive – "I get to determine unilaterally which words in what order will set the terms through which the experience shall occur."

THE POETRY

> "The poem heard, the poem seen, the poem thought."
> – Webb, *Nothing But Brush Strokes*

As epigraph to "Falling Glass," her section of *Trio,* which also contains poems by Gael Turnbull and Eli Mandel, Webb chose a quotation from Louis MacNeice's "Bagpipe Music": "The glass is falling hour by hour, the glass will fall forever, / But if you break the bloody glass you won't hold up the weather." Obviously, the social, economic, emotional, and psychological outlook in *Trio* and in *Even Your Right Eye* (which contains eleven poems from *Trio*) is often storm-wracked, "… Is Our Distress," "Pain," and "Lament" arc over these first two volumes. But pain, the poet declares, "throws a bridge of value to belief" in the same way that death, the dark ground of life, necessitates our search for enlightenment, for meaning, the ultimate value whether it leads "towards or away from" belief. Other poems in both books clearly reflect Webb's preoccupation with the nature of suffering, social and personal. Lacking the ontological security Laing speaks of, she engaged early the struggle to find meaning for herself. But these early volumes are not all Sturm und Drang. The intense drive to reach for light beyond the storm is transformed into poems like "To a Zen Buddhist Who Laughs Daily"; the pun-filled "Double Entendre"; the leisurely "Sunday Morning Walk" Webb takes in London's Kensington Gardens; "Standing (*for Earle Birney*)," one of her initial essays in projective verse or field poetry; and "Earth Descending," which for Webb was "a turning-point poem" with what she calls "cosmic" implications. These implications lead us, eventually, to "'A Model of the Universe,'" and to other poems in which we are challenged by "Chaos science," "Particle Physics," and the "immense smallness" of "superstrings" in *Hanging Fire*. "Earth Descending" is, essentially, a victory song, a song of liberation:

> I am free from the sun's orbit
> and morbid regulated glances daily,
> and free also from the moon's nightly
> slightly sickening romances …

The mischievous off-kilter and internal rhymes – orbit / morbid, glances / romances, nightly / slightly – operate like musical markings and establish the poem's tempo and tone. "This is the end," she shouts in triumph. "No need to belabour the point, however." She chose this poem, which Browning might have called "a dramatic lyric," to sound the final note of her second volume. In many ways it marks the end of her apprenticeship. Her most famous poem in *Even Your Right Eye* is undoubtedly the much anthologized "Marvell's Garden." Its impassioned wit and intellectualized emotion owe a great deal to the Metaphysical Poets – here, to the elegant Marvell; in other poems, to the more roughshod Donne. Their presences hover like distant eminences in the landscape of Webb's poetry, just below the horizon.

The Sea Is Also a Garden offers a greater variety of poetic forms, modes, voices, colours, and tones than the first two volumes; but the "destroying dust" in "Countered," the war which is "architecture for aggression" in "Breaking," and "the chemic sun" in "Bomb Shelter" reveal Webb's constant awareness of the larger world in the late 1940s and early 1950s, reminding readers that these poems were written in the shadow of the mushroom cloud and the Cold War. Nevertheless, she rises to perfection for the first time in this book. "Propositions" is a truly great poem: "That's one of the miracles," says Webb. "It was written very quickly" (Ruzesky, 229). It takes off from the earlier "A Walk by the Seine" (in *Even Your Right Eye*):

> But you and I slowing
> our words to a muted tone
> (for beauty silences the horse-drawn
> carriages of wisdom), meshing
> light and leaves in that imperial notion
> of stasis and dream, move and stand,
> like love and death, at the river's edge.

"Propositions" begins:

> I could divide a leaf
> and give you half.
>
> Or I could search for two leaves
> sending you one.
>
> Or I could walk to the river
> and look across

and seeing you there,
or not there,

absence or presence,
would spring the balance to my day.

Six more couplets sustain without faltering the pristine lyricism of the poem. Perhaps we "could speed four eyes, / the chariot horses of our dreams and visions," says the ecstatic poet who ends by proposing a "hand sketching in the air / a half-moon, its hidden wholeness there." So many of Webb's best poems do just that: sketch a half that implies a hidden whole. It is one of the techniques she devised early in her career and put to brilliant use over the next three and half decades.

Naked Poems, her fourth volume, is a perfect case in point. It consists of a series – two "suites" – of love poems, followed by "Non Linear," thirteen discrete lyrics announcing, among many other things, the birth of "a new alphabet" with which to create a new (for Webb) poetic language: the minimalist language of *Naked Poems* born at exactly the same time as Philip Glass's minimalist music for a 1965 production of Beckett's *Comédie.* An ironic "Suite of Lies" (though lies are rarely sweet) and "Some final questions" complete this exquisite book, elegantly designed by the Japanese-Canadian artist Takao Tanabe. The painful but playful interrogation of the final section, in which Webb's mastery of the conversational tone is forever established, ends with an enigmatic "*Oh?*" A zero? The fifteenth letter of the (new?) alphabet looking like a (w)hole? Or merely an impertinent echo of the poet's last word?

Listen. If I have known beauty
let's say I came to it
asking

Webb's technique of proposing a half but implying a whole is particularly relevant to the opening suites of love poems. Pauline Butling admonishes Frank Davey and me for not pointing out in our writings on *Naked Poems* that the first two suites are in fact lesbian love poems. As Webb herself told Williamson, although she was "very successful in evasive techniques" in writing these (and other) poems, "for anyone who studies them closely, it's perfectly obvious … How anyone could read it ['the lesbian love affair'] without knowing, I don't understand." "The blouse gives it away," as Williamson rightly observes (329–30). Reviewing Butling's book, the more critically sensitive Keith, writes:

Primarily, I would argue, these are love poems. Certainly, they arise out of a "lesbian context" but the restraint and delicacy of the relationship are not confined to such a context. (Consider Shakespeare's "Shall I compare thee to a summer's day," which is only limited by reference to the homoerotic.) *Naked Poems* can speak eloquently to readers for whom lesbianism is remote. Butling's students who, she tells us, tend to "assume they are heterosexual love poems" ... are assuredly ignoring the details, but may well be right (on their own terms) in responding to the love rather than the lesbianism.

In a recent letter, Webb says: "there has been too much interest in my lesbian side when the most significant relationships have been with men. Many more men in my life than women, though perhaps it would have been better the other way around. It all seems so far away now" (Letter, July 2013).

Wilson's Bowl was not published until 1980, fifteen years after *Naked Poems*. This is what Kamboureli calls one of those "periods of silence" that have become "almost mythologized" by Webb's critics. The hidden wholeness of the truth is, of course, very different from the half-truths sketched by those who haven't done their research. The poet herself explains: "in that fertile silence I am hearing many things and taking in a great deal, so that it doesn't necessarily feel like silence to me. It's just silent from the performance point of view. It requires silence to hear, and I suppose that is a very important aspect of the whole process." In the first place, from 1964 to 1969 Webb was working full time at the CBC and she was working particularly hard to maintain the high standard of *Ideas*. Though she found little time to write during this period and confessed, "I feel my life is desperately empty and the destroyer is at work" (Letter, February 6, 1966), in fact, some of the famous figures who appeared on *Ideas* – Paul Goodman, for example, R.D. Laing, N.O. Brown, and Glenn Gould – stimulated Webb's mind and imagination, helping generate ideas of her own, materials that would sooner or later be transformed into new poems. She first became interested in anarchism "by reading Paul Goodman's novel, *The Empire City*, published in 1959." Goodman was one of "the remarkable American anarchists of the twentieth century." His presence on the program reactivated her socialist interests. "I thought I must go and find out more about anarchism and Kropotkin [who] was often spoken of in the novel."

Which is exactly what she did. Suffering from nervous exhaustion, Webb took a leave of absence from the CBC in 1967 and flew back to the West Coast where, for the first time since her childhood, she stayed on Salt Spring Island. As the "Kropotkin Note Books, 1967–69" prove, she had already started to think about and write poems she hoped might be part of a larger work centring on the life of the Russian anarchist Kropotkin. Before returning to Toronto, she visited Russia. In *Wilson's Bowl*, the Kropotkin poems are clearly dated 1967. A report to the Canada Council establishes the fact that almost all the poems in the "Portraits" and "Crimes" sections of *Wilson's Bowl* were completed by 1970–71. More poems, including the bitter "Antisong," "Solitary Confinement," and "Letters to Margaret Atwood" belong to 1973; "Lines from Gwen [MacEwen]. Lines for Ben [Metcalfe]," to 1975. In 1977, Lilo Berliner, a relatively new fellow-islander and friend of Webb's, committed suicide. She was, says Webb, "passionately interested in Northwest Coast Indian art, particularly petroglyphs." Shown "a small bowl or basin, carved into a rock on the beach near her 'Zen house'," Berliner instantly dedicated it to Wilson Duff, the distinguished professor of anthropology at UBC. She called it "Wilson's Bowl," thus initiating the composition of the "Artifacts" section and providing the title of Webb's next volume. Although fifteen years had elapsed since the appearance of *Naked Poems,* Webb had been far from unproductive – apart from a short period in the 1960s when she was too busy and too exhausted to write poetry and another in which she retreated to lick her wounds after reading John Bentley Mays's vituperative critical attack on her work in *Open Letter* (1973): "I was genuinely pained and damaged by the Bentley Mays article."

"This book has been long in coming," Webb states in the foreword to *Wilson's Bowl.* True, but it was certainly worth waiting for. It not only confirmed her pre-eminent place in Canadian poetry, it also demonstrated more powerfully than before the extraordinary range of her work: subject matter, poetic forms and voices, versatility of techniques. Even though the eight Kropotkin poems represent only a small part of a larger unwritten but imagined whole, they have about them something grand, like scenes from an unfinished opera or oratorio: "Whose love, tell me, O love's divine airs / elaborates the oratorio?" Love's "divine airs" float us back to the line from Donne's "The Ecstasy" – "Else a great prince in prison lies" – linking political prisoner in solitary confinement to private man, Peter, growing old: "Who did he lust for or sleep with / and who shifted his decorous sweetness into plain-song / pain-song, body to body?" The final words in "from *The Kropotkin Poems*" might well be a chorale that closes the incomplete work: "O love words flow / on love whose airs are his own oratorio. // In Adam's garden / he plants all his blood."

At the other end of the scale from the Kropotkin poems is the light-fingered lyricism of "Metaphysics of Spring" and the wryly divine comedy of the Audenesque "Composed Like Them" with its several allusions to Dante. The title is a quotation from Auden's "September 1, 1939":

May I composed like them [the Just]
Of Eros and of dust,
Beleaguered by the same
Negation and despair,
Show an affirming flame.

(A wish or a prayer Webb herself might well have uttered.) Webb's stanza form echoes that of the Auden poem; and the first two lines of the fifth stanza – "Is this what Auden knew, / that the pair are secretly bored" – allude to another Auden poem which begins "At last the secret is out, as it must always come in the end." It continues, "Under the look of fatigue, the attack of migraine and the sigh / There is always another story, there is more than meets the eye." Which thought accords with my theory of Webb's poetics of "hidden wholeness." As Webb herself puts it, "One of my habitual techniques in life" – and in art, we might add – "is to remain ambivalent, ambiguous, mysterious … not going around being easily labelled or identified is my refusal to be uncomplex or oversimplified and nailed down or up." And of course Auden is right about secrets coming out in the end. Webb's poem is a witty and affectionate tribute to P.K. Page, to whom it was originally dedicated and who slyly appears in the reference to "Pat Bay."

So many major poems appear in Webb's 1980 volume, it's hard to pass any by without comment: the Bergman-like homage to "Rilke," whom Webb claims as "my spiritual guide and mentor (one good narcissist deserves another)"; the wild epistolary prose-poems "to Margaret Atwood," which anticipate *Hanging Fire's* apocalypse; and "The Days of the Unicorns," another of those "miracle" poems like "Propositions." The magisterial "A Question of Questions" is a major work, and the complex "Artifacts" section rightly forms the book's climactic centre. Often enigmatic ("I riddle my enterprise"), this sequence grew out of the correspondence between Lilo Berliner and the famous anthropologist Wilson Duff, who committed suicide in 1976. Berliner left a package of letters on Webb's doorstep before walking into the sea and drowning herself in 1977. "She was a seeker after signs and symbols," says Webb. "Given to Zen-like insights and absurdities, she was also addicted to Jungian archetypes, dreams and synchronicities." An unpublished villanelle by Webb anticipates the opening riddle of "Wilson's Bowl":

Keep that intact by luck that's unrefined:
toss coins, risk dice, pull out the golden straw
when on the path you see the twigs aligned.

"Wilson's Bowl":

> "You may read my signs
> but I cross my path
> and show you nothing
> on your way."

The second poem in "Artifacts" is a "Found Poem" incorporating quotations from Federico García Lorca's lecture "Play and Theory of the *Duende*" (1933). Webb's found poem is a synecdoche since the whole section is, in a sense, a found poem: found on Webb's doorstep. Resistant to any simple definition, *duende* is a goblin, a spirit, a fiercely intense state of emotion (St. Teresa's ecstasy), that which is heard in the *cante jondo,* the dark or deep songs of Andalusia: "*duende* does not come unless he sees that death is possible." The last word of the poem, "*Tremendum,*" appears in the "*Dies Irae*" of the Mass; it also takes us back to Webb's 1971 CBC radio program on "The Question as an Instrument of Torture" in which she alludes to "the voice from the Whirlwind in the Book of Job," a voice that might be seen / heard as the *duende.* Webb quotes Kenneth Rexroth on the subject: "The Speech of the Almighty is a parade of power, devoid of moral content, but intolerably charged with the *tremendum,* the awe and judgement of the utterly other." Obviously, Webb's "Found Poem" refers the reader back to the Kropotkin poems and to "A Question of Questions."

Why, Webb asked herself in 1969, did I become interested in "the question of questions?" Because, to hazard a guess, it was inevitable. Webb the questioning child, the adult philosopher who asked a more probing kind of question in her search for meaning, was bound, sooner or later, to question the question itself. This is why I call it "magisterial." It is a master poem in that it provides the key to much of Webb's poetry. It reveals the central struggle in Webb's life and in her art: the quest for a master – a "*Zen Master,*" perhaps – who will not attempt to master her but will teach her how to master both herself and her art. Dating from 1970, "A Question of Questions" is a kind of Socratic dialogue in which the self interrogates the self about the nature of desire – sexual desire as the desire *to know.* In her 1971 program on "The Question as an Instrument of Torture," Webb wonders if Dostoevsky in the Grand Inquisitor's scene of *The Brothers Karamazov* consciously transformed "the devil's temptation of Christ into three questions" or "was it a moment of poetic inspiration in which he grasped the hooked dialectic between the silent prisoner and the loquacious Inquisitor?" in this poem, Webb plays both the not so silent prisoner *and* the inquisitor:

question
query
hook
    of the soul
    a question of
questions
....
    and who are you in this
school
room
torture chamber
    whose are you?
    and what of your
    trials and errors?
the judge
    in his echo chamber
    cannot know
    and nor can you
    you cannot answer

Does the "Succulent lobe of the ear / droplet of flesh" – itself resembling the lower part of the question mark – does it hear the self-questioner, "Does it know what I say?" What the questioned / questioning self wants to hear is not another question but a greeting:

Hello / hello is as equal as we'll come
                    my love
            my question
        my answer
              smiles on one side,
    ugly, or other of
            power and seduction.

"Love, mastery and freedom" Webb declared to be "the heart of the matter," in a series of five poetry programs aired on CBC in 1966 (LAC). Love and seduction, mastery and power are obviously related. The self's search for freedom from desire – the desire to know – from "our voluptuous questing," provides the intellectual basis of this densely textured poem. "Thinking, at best, / is dreaming / chase and quarry." The mini-drama of Section Four was inspired by the story of "Odette" (Brailly-Sansom-Churchill), sent as a spy to Nazi-occupied France in the Second World War. She was captured, tortured, sentenced to death but sent to Ravensbrook concentration camp – which she survived.

The final section of this master poem is dedicated to R.D. Laing with whom Webb worked on *Ideas*. It opens and closes with unmistakable echoes of a passage in Laing's *The Self and Others*:

> The error lies in
> the state of desire
> in wanting the answers
>
> ....
>
> *Zen Master.*

> The dominant fantasy in a group may be that the therapist has "the answer," and that if they had "the answer" they would not suffer. The therapist's task is then, like the Zen Master's, to point out that suffering is not due to not getting "the answer," but is the very state of desire that assumes the existence of that kind of answer, and the frustration of not getting it.

Laing, a controversial psychiatrist in his day, is a trickster like Webb herself. He becomes, perhaps, her "deceiving angel's / in-shadow" threatening to fly off with her head. Headless (unable to think), she recalls a headless Indian petroglyph "painted in red." The red-crested woodpecker that appears at the end of the poem is a bird with a handsome head – pecking away at the tree of the knowledge of good and evil? He's also an avatar of Laing, the Zen Master –

> dazzling all questions
> out of me, amazement
> and outbreathing
> become a form
> of my knowing.

Water and Light: Ghazals and Anti Ghazals contains very different forms of knowing from those in *Wilson's Bowl*. Much has been written about Webb's discovery and use of the ghazal, the putative verse form adopted in this her seventh volume of poetry (not counting the two volumes of *Selected Poems*). She approaches "the ghazal tradition more as bricoleur than disciple," Douglas Barbour rightly points out. Technically speaking, Webb's anti ghazal owes little to the very complex lyric commonly found in Persian, Urdu, Arabic, Turkish, and Pashto literatures. As Webb herself said in a 1985 poetry reading, "the anti ghazals are disobedient to the inherent conventionality of the form." The unrhymed couplet in various numerical sets is not uncommon in poetry in English: George Bowering's "The House," Ted Hughes's "The River," and, most importantly, Wallace Stevens's *The Man with the Blue Guitar* composed in sets of five, six, or seven couplets. What distinguishes Webb's anti ghazal, inspired less by Ghalib than by John Thompson's *Stilt Jack* and Adrienne Rich's translations of some ghazals of Ghalib, is the discreteness of each couplet. Supposedly, it has no logical or syntactical connection with the couplet that follows. In point of fact, many of these poems do *enjambe* from one couplet to the next. Furthermore, a unity of idea often surprises the reader ("the hidden wholeness" again) because it depends, not on syntax or overt subject matter, but on sound effects or the relation between ostensibly diverse objects (as in much metaphysical poetry) or even on a simple allusion. This is a fine example:

> My loves are dying. Or is it that my love
> is dying, day by day, brief life, brief candle,
>
> a flame, *flambeau*, torch, alive, singing
> somewhere in the shadow: Here, this way, here.
>
> Hear the atoms ambling, the genes a-tick
> in grandfather's clock, in the old bones of beach.
>
> Sun on the Sunday water in November.
> Dead leaves on wet ground. The ferry leaves on time.
>
> Time in your flight – O – a wristwatch strapped
> to my heart, ticking erratically, winding down.

The dazzling array of sound effects play together like a well-directed chamber orchestra. But, in addition, the brilliant, brief allusion to Shakespeare's "brief candle" in *Macbeth* unifies the whole poem. Macbeth's Act V soliloquy – "She should have died hereafter. / There would have been a time for such a word. / Tomorrow, and tomorrow, and tomorrow, / Creeps in this petty pace from day to day / To the last syllable of recorded time … Out, out, brief candle!" – harmonizes Webb's ghazal in a wonderfully musical way, making us feel as we do in opera when two characters perform a duet, singing *different* lyrics to the *same* melody. We move from candle, an ancient form of timekeeper, to clock to wristwatch (the O between the two dashes looking exactly like a wristwatch laid flat on a counter). We are winding down from month to day to hour, like the "poor player / That struts and frets his hour upon the stage / And then is heard no more." The ferry, doubtless under the command of Captain Charon, leaves "on time." *O Time in Your Flight* (another allusion, here to Hubert Evans's 1979 novel), forever at our back like Marvell's "wingéd chariot." What is so extraordinary about this poem – and all the others in this volume that glitter like Sunday sunlight on water – is the lightness of tone that belies the richness of texture. After "Sunday Water: Thirteen Anti Ghazals" comes a section called "The Birds" in which we find the peacock – "the colour of chaos was not // Peacock blue." What follows is a series of eight poems entitled "I Daniel," yet another of Webb's miracles, dense, dramatic, enigmatic as all apocalyptic texts are. "Frivolities," in which "Phyllis" and her alter ego "Fishstar" make an appearance, fade into the "Middle Distance," the final section of this splendid book. No wonder Webb has confessed that *Water and Light* and *Naked Poems* are her two "best" and "most satisfactory" books. But what a shock to hear her describe both as "very minimalist book[s]"! *Water and Light* seems anything but; it's such a rich deposit of dazzling poetic ideas and effects. Webb, however, explains what she means: "I seem to write one raggedy book … where the poems are different kinds and different lengths and not totally pure. And then I go into this very economical form and the result *is* aesthetically pure." And in this sense "minimalist."

Hanging Fire is one of her "raggedy" books. "I call these poems my uglies," Webb told Kamboureli. Presumably she calls them ugly because some are full of rage: "this book is much angrier than any of my other books." For example, "'Temporal Lobe'" starts with a migraine:

> one outgrows them, they say.
> But today.
> Writhings, rage clenches
> my fist. Frozen pea bag
> smashes against the hearth.

Not only anger, but also fear, disaster, and distress crowd into other poems. Asked about the volume title, Webb replied "it means 'holding your fire', literally." Ordered to hold his fire, a gunner knows not to fire – yet. Webb also referred to "'Krakatoa'," the second poem in the book; specifically, to the line "my held-back fire." Then she recalled the firebombing of Dresden and a "*curtain* of fire." Dresden became for her "an image of the disaster that I've always seen coming." The disaster is holding back and yet, like the fire curtain, already hanging in the air, happening now. Sonja Skarstedt asked if the image is part of Webb's "apocalyptic vision?" "Yes, my apocalyptic view. The apocalypse has *not* come and I have been expecting it ever since I was a teenager." Apocalypse envisions an end to time, transforming *chronos* into *kairos* as I explain in my article on *Hanging Fire*. "Webb's Book of Revelation: Lifting the Lid Off 'Krakatoa' and 'Spiritual Storm'" explores at some length the apocalyptic nature of the poet's vision in this book, which falls, like apocalypse itself, into three parts, "*Tour de Force*," "Hanging Fire," and "Scattered Effects." Punning on "*Tour de Force*," Webb explains that in this section she is "mainly working with violence … And reactions to violence. Power and force. *Force*, perhaps, more than power. Tour de *force!*" Of "Scattered Effects" she remarks, "you know, what you do after the dead have died, their effects are scattered."

Maybe these facts help account for what Webb calls the "non-reception" of *Hanging Fire*. Maybe it struck some readers as too dark, too grim after the bright, water-sprightliness of the previous volume. But, like *Trio* and *Even Your Right Eye*, it is not all doom and gloom. "Cat & Mouse Game" exemplifies perfectly the kind of humour to be found in this volume; the poet is playing cat-and-mouse games with the reader throughout. As epigraph, Webb quotes from Daphne Marlatt's *musing with mothertongue:*

> in poetry … sound will initiate thought by a process of association. words call each other up, evoke each other, provoke each other, nudge each other into utterance … a form of thought that is not rational but erotic because it works by attraction. a drawing, a pulling toward. a "liking."

A "form of thought … not rational but erotic because it works by attraction": this is a crucial point here. Some of Webb's most overtly erotic poems appear in this book. Words are provocative agents, and some of them, as Webb explains in her prefatory note, are also "given": "Titles of poems in quotation marks are 'given' words, phrases, or sentences that arrive unbidden in my head." These given words provoke and attract others and, by erotic association, call into "beauteous being" the kind of utterance that characterizes *Hanging Fire*. It may well be Webb's angriest but it is also one of her most musical books; not musical in the way that Keats and Tennyson are – mellifluous – but more in the manner of Donne or Robert Duncan, highly syncopated rhythmically with elusive wisps of melody. The poems resound with allusions to Wagner's *Flying Dutchman,* Samuel Barber's *Adagio for Strings,* Stravinsky's *Firebird,* Philip Glass's *Satyagraha* (Webb's poem "The Salt Tax" is in fact a sound poem), Leoncavallo's *Pagliacci,* Paul Horn, Bach, "holy ghosts fiddling / while the planets burn," "old hoedown / razzmatazz," "Flamenco, castanets' death / rattle," "'Evensong'," and many other musical terms. "'Evensong'," subtitled "(even song syllabics)," perversely consists of an odd number of lines (nineteen), each of which contains an odd number of syllables (nine) and it opens with a musical pun: "Tending toward music, the artist's / life tends toward solitary notes …" Full of phonic fun, despite the sometimes tough subject matter, the violent images, the apocalyptic vision, *Hanging Fire* concludes with "The Making of a Japanese Print," four of Webb's most stunning lyric poems which are also, angrily and triumphantly, her most overt feminist statement.

The final section of *Peacock Blue* contains poems previously uncollected and, in some cases, unpublished. "I shall be single," the poem the poet has chosen to place at the beginning of this volume, is one of the previously unpublished works. The rest range in date from 1951 to 2001, from "Involution," her first poem to be published in a well-known poetry magazine (*Northern Review*), to "Maureen Reading." (Because it is simply too occasional, Webb declined to publish the "Selected Poem" she wrote for Sharon Thesen in 2007.) Fifty years separate first poem and last. What comes in between represents *in parvo* Webb's entire career as poet. The poetic voices and the *personae* they assume in these poems are as extensive as those we find in the eight published volumes: sonnet, villanelle, elegy, simple lyric ("Birds" and "pearl poem"), anecdotal lyric ("Crosswords" and "'Revision'"), lyric and dramatic monologue ("Richard II," originally one of Webb's "Portraits," and "The Tree Speaks"), playful occasional poems ("Astronaut"), satire, parody, and poems of outspoken social protest ("Continuum," "How the Indians Got Left Out of the Business of Patriating the Constitution"), as well as the beautiful prose-poem "Sitting, 1982."

Webb has said, more than once, that she held back her anger for many, many years: anger at all kinds of social injustice – women's long history of oppression, all forms of prejudice and, most understandably, her own passivity. Of the woman who emerges, cursing, in "The Making of a Japanese Print," she observes, "I have only recently learned how to do that in my work. I've done it in my life, but I have not been able to get it into my work until recently. I think that's a big advance in *Hanging Fire* – that my anger really comes through, and I'm able to curse." That "Little Lines," the very early, unpublished poem, should so clearly anticipate her final volume is, perhaps, something of a surprise:

> I turn my hand
> into a soft fist
> turning away wrath
> holding my own anger
> softly like a moth
> in the curved palm.

We hear that held-back anger again in her "What Is to Be Done Poem":

> The denial of one's neighbour is
> easy / as
> denial of one's self / the me
> -keeping silence.

And again in "Sitting, 1982":

> These pears have never heard of Amnesty International.
> But even better they have never heard of torture, mass
> executions, etc., etc. They are just lying here, lolling here,
> casually emitting the perfume of pure pear as I try to gather
> myself together. They don't want to be touched so I don't
> touch them. I sit and wait for them to move.

The pain, the existential angst, the often mordant humour which mark so much of Webb's work are all in evidence in this final section of the book. In "Involution," Sisyphus, Camus's symbol of the absurdity of life's pointless repetitions, is "chained to his own eye's prison // gaoled to a goal of stone." In another poem, "Rabbits Intimidate Her Eyes ...", "in love with barrenness," the poet flies from "this / diseased increase." Lovers, like "Idiot Birds," "strut / in our summer of despair" and discover that "We are the children of the love we made" ("Sonnet"). "Living / alone may not be tidy," the poet admits; but in "A Room of One's Own":

> Lying alone on the bed
> and dreaming in the drift
> of heavy poems –
> Dante, Homer, ambivalent Joyce –
> I lie in a comfortable close

The poet's whimsicality is also present in "New Year Message for J. Alfred Prufrock" and her "Intuition of a Literary Weekend":

> So toot your own horn dearie
> the weary River Cataraqui
> can't be fenced unless we form a claque,
> we form a claque, a clique, a brick-a-brackerie
> and all go down with Moses
> All Go Down!

"I don't suppose I would have written poetry if I hadn't had a good ear. I've often said that when I write a poem 'I play by ear' – which I did when I played the piano long ago. A way of composing poems, crooning along ... reciting it over and over, if only in my head, until I thought I'd got it right." Webb's unerring command of sound effects is to be heard in many of these uncollected and unpublished poems: for example, in "Weather Forecast," "Dust into Dust," a poem that introduces us to her clever and characteristic use of repetition, and "'Mirrored Room' in the Albright-Knox," another of her famous glass poems, every bit as bright and brittle as the better known glass trio in *The Sea Is Also a Garden.*

"Involution" is remarkable for its incorporation of the Sisyphus myth. Apart from this poem, and the much later "'Psychopomp'," which centres on Hermes / Mercury in his function as guide, leading the dead across into Hades, myths do not have a place in Webb work. "I do not want mythological figures in my poems, especially as subjects, foregrounding, subjecting personages." Raven, dark and holy, flaps into and out of *Wilson's Bowl*; and the Manitou, spirit beings of the Algonquin peoples, stand silent and alone in "'Ignis Fatuus'" (*Hanging Fire*). But for the most part, Webb prefers to reside in "the land / of only what is." However, one recurrent figure deserves notice: "star fish // fish star" sounds like a little moment of wordplay / foreplay at the start of *Naked Poems*. In *Water and Light,* the other volume to which the ever self-critical Webb gives her least qualified approval, Fishstar pops up unexpectedly and assumes the function of Webb's alter ego (the poet's use of a pseudonym is part of the ghazal tradition):

> Peacock blue. Words fail me,
> *Fishstar,* for the packed, inbred
>
> splendour of this bird.

In fact, a friend of Webb's owned two peacocks, Elizabeth and Essex. Blinded by the brilliant colours, the "blue-green scream" of the male for his mate, it is suddenly "the first morning // of creation, an absurd idea"; but "I tell you, / *Fishstar,* the colour of chaos was not // Peacock blue." Fishstar appears again later, writing on yellow paper:

> Whose song is this anyway?
> Is it a song being sung
>
> on the narrow road to the North?

"Oh *Fishstar!*" the poet exclaims but Fishstar is suddenly silent. No more answers to all the questions. Half hidden within this odd name ("Starfish" would be more commonplace) is the wholeness of Ishtar, the Assyrian, Babylonian goddess, worshipped as the goddess of love, sexuality (her cult included sacred prostitution), fertility – and war. Because her symbol was the eight-pointed star identified with Venus, appearing sometimes in the east (Hesper), sometimes in the west (Vesper), Ishtar was seen as unpredictable. A *femme fatale* (she killed her lover Tammuz) and given to terrible rages, she nevertheless incarnates creativity in her ability to draw together so many opposites (the imagination described by Coleridge in his *Biographia Literaria*). The star of the sea, *Stella maris,* is a jellyfish with a sting that burns (*Cnidaria*), distinct from the starfish (*Asteroidea*). Says a character in Margaret Drabble's *The Radiant Way* (1987), "'*stella marina,* the fish that burns like a star in the midst of the water, the starfish that burns at the North Pole'" (347). Fishstar, such an innocent seeming figure – another half-moon sketched in the evening air – burns in the sea which is also a garden and hangs fire, if not at the North Pole, then certainly on the narrow road north of the forty-ninth parallel.

JOHN F. HULCOOP
Vancouver, November 2013–February 2014

Works Cited

Adorno, Theodor. *Prisms*. Translated by Shierry Weber Nicholsen and Samuel Weber. Cambridge, MA: MIT Press, 1983. First published as *Prismen: Kulturkritik und Gesellschaft*. Berlin: Suhrkamp Verlag, 1955. References are to the MIT Press edition.

Auden, W.H. *Collected Shorter Poems 1930–1944*. London: Faber & Faber, 1950.

Barbour, Douglas. "Naked Poems." In *Canadian Encyclopedia*. 2000 ed. Toronto: McClelland and Stewart, 1999. Also available online.

_____. *Lyric / Anti-lyric: Essays on Contemporary Poetry*. Edmonton: NeWest Press, 2001.

Barthes, Roland. "The Death of the Author," (1968). In *Image / Music / Text*. Translated by Stephen Heath. Hill and Wang, 1977. References are to the Hill and Wang edition.

Beckett, Samuel. *The Complete Short Prose, 1929-1989*. Edited by S.E. Gontarski. New York: Grove Press, 1995, 109.

Butling, Pauline. *Seeing in the Dark: The Poetry of Phyllis Webb*. Waterloo, ON: Wilfred Laurier UP, 1997.

_____, ed. "You Devise. We Devise." *A Festschrift for Phyllis Webb*. West Coast Line 25.3 (Winter 1991-92). Referred to as "*Festschrift*."

Collis, Stephen. *Phyllis Webb and the Common Good: Poetry / Anarchy / Abstraction*. Vancouver: Talonbooks, 2007.

Davey, Frank. *From Here to There*. Victoria and Toronto: Press Porcépic, 1974.

Drabble, Margaret. *The Radiant Way: A Novel*. Toronto: McClelland and Stewart, 1987.

Epstein, Joseph. "Who Killed Poetry?" *Commentary* (August 1988): 13–20.

Frye, Northrop. Back dust-jacket. *Wilson's Bowl* by Phyllis Webb. Toronto: Coach House, 1980.

Gioia, Dana. "Can Poetry Matter?" *The Atlantic Monthly* (May 1991): 94–106.

Hayman, Raymond. *Artaud and After*. Oxford: Oxford UP, 1977.

Hulcoop, John. "Phyllis Webb and the Priestess of Motion." *Canadian Literature* 32 (Spring 1967): 29–39.

_____. Interview with Phyllis Webb. CBC Radio. Produced by John Merritt. 1980.

_____. "Webb's Book of Revelation: Lifting the Lid Off 'Krakatoa' and 'Spiritual Storm.'" In *Inside the Poem: Essays and Poems in Honour of Donald M. Stephens*. Edited by W.H. New. Toronto: Oxford UP, 1992. 230–45.

_____. "Coming to Love, Asking." *Trek: The Magazine of the University of British Columbia* (Spring 2002): 14–17.

Kamboureli, Smaro. "Seeking Shape, Seeking Meaning: An Interview with Phyllis Webb." "You Devise. We Devise." *A Festschrift for Phyllis Webb*. Edited by Pauline Butling. *West Coast Line* 25.3 (Winter 1991-92): 21–41.

Keats, John. "Ode to a Nightingale." In *The Poetical Works of John Keats*. Edited by and with introduction by H. Buxton Forman. Oxford: Oxford UP, 1948.

Keith, W.J. "Phyllis Webb, Reader Trouble, and Gender Trouble." Review of Pauline Butling's *Seeing in the Dark: The Poetry of Phyllis Webb*. *Canadian Poetry* 43 (1998): 132–43.

Laing, R.D. *The Self and Others*. Harmondsworth, UK: Pelican, 1961.

Lorca, Federico García. *In Search of Duende: Prose Selections*. Edited and translated by Christopher Maurer. New York: New Directions Bibelot, 1998.

Marshall, Tom. *Harsh and Lovely Land: The Major Canadian Poets and the Making of a Canadian Tradition*. Vancouver: University of British Columbia Press, 1979.

Mays, John Bentley. "Phyllis Webb (for Bob Wallace)." *Open Letter* 2.6 (Fall 1973): 8–33.

McKinnon, Barry. *The Death of a Lyric Poet: Poems and Drafts*. Prince George, BC: Caledonia Writing Series, 1975.

Munton, Anne. "Excerpt from an Interview with Phyllis Webb." *West Coast Line* 25.3 (Winter 1991–2): 81–85.

Perloff, Marjorie. "Language Poets and the Lyric Subject: Ron Silliman's *Albany* and Susan Howe's *Buffalo*." Electronic Poetry Center. Internet. 1998.

Ruzesky, Jay. "Peek-a-boo." In *Where the Words Come From: Canadian Poets in Conversation*. Edited by Tim Bowling. Roberts Creek, BC: Nightwood Editions, 2002.

Sappho. 48: "The moon has set ..." In *Greek Lyric, Volume 1: Sappho and Alcaeus*. Translated and edited by David A. Campbell. Cambridge, MA: Harvard UP, 1990.

Shakespeare, William. *Macbeth. The Works of William Shakespeare*. Edited by W.G. Clark and W.A. Wright. London: Macmillan, 1949.

Sieghart, William. "Popularizing Poetry in the UK." Updated by Tim Love. Internet. 2010.

Skarstedt, Sonja A. Review of *Hanging Fire*: An Interview with Phyllis Webb." *Zymergy* 5.1 (Spring 1991): 35–49.

Stephens, Wallace. "Adagio." In *Opus Posthumous*. Edited and with an introduction by Samuel French Morse. New York: Knopf, 1957.

Sujir, Leila. "Addressing a Presence: An Interview with Phyllis Webb." *Prairie Fire* 9.1 (Spring 1988): 30–43.

Vendler, Helen. *Wallace Stevens: Words Chosen Out of Desire*. Cambridge, MA, and London: Harvard UP, 1984.

Wachtel, Eleanor. "Intimations of Immortality." *Books in Canada* 12 (November 1983): 8–15.

Webb, Phyllis, Gael Turnbull, and E.W. Mandel. *Trio: First Poems by Gael Turnbull, Phyllis Webb, and E.W. Mandel*. Preface by Louis Dudek. Toronto: Contact, 1954. Referred to as "*Trio*."

Webb, Phyllis. *Even Your Right Eye*. Toronto: McClelland & Stewart, 1956. Referred to as "*EYRE*."

_____. *The Sea Is Also a Garden*. Toronto: Ryerson, 1962. Referred to as "*SEAG*."

_____. *Naked Poems*. Vancouver: Periwinkle, 1965. Referred to as "*NP*."

_____. *Selected Poems of Phyllis Webb, 1954–65*. Vancouver: Talonbooks, 1971. Referred to as "*SP*."

_____. "Phyllis Webb's Canada." Essay first published in *MacLean's*, October 1971. Republished in *Nothing But Brush Strokes: Selected Prose*. Edmonton: NeWest, 1995. 105–110.

_____. "Protest in Paradise." *Maclean's*. June 1973.

_____. *Wilson's Bowl*. Toronto: Coach House, 1980. Referred to as *"WB."*

_____. *Sunday Water: Thirteen Anti Ghazals*. Lantzville, BC: Island Writing Series, 1982. Referred to as *"SW."*

_____. *Talking*. Dunvegan, ON: Quadrant Editions, 1982. Referred to as *"T."*

_____. "The Question as an Instrument of Torture." *Talking*. Montreal: Quadrant, 1982. 31–45.

_____. *The Vision Tree: Selected Poems by Phyllis Webb*. Vancouver: Talonbooks, 1982. Referred to as *"VT."*

_____. *Water and Light: Ghazals and Anti Ghazals. Poems*. Toronto: Coach House, 1984. Referred to as *"WL."*

_____. *Hanging Fire*. Toronto: Coach House, 1990. Referred to as *"HF."*

_____. "Phyllis Webb and Daphne Marlatt: A Selected Correspondence." *West Coast Line* 25.3 (Winter 1991-92): 89–94.

_____. "Poetry and Psychobiography." Lecture delivered to the Vancouver Institute, March 13, 1993. University of British Columbia Archives phonotape 1891. Sound recording. Published in *Nothing But Brush Strokes: Selected Prose*. Edmonton: NeWest, 1995.

_____. *Nothing But Brush Strokes: Selected Prose*. Edmonton: NeWest, 1995. Referred to as *"NBBS."*

_____. Correspondence with John Hulcoop. Various dates. Library and Archives Canada. LMS-0236. John Hulcoop Fonds, 1950–2000. Referred to as "Letter," plus date.

_____. Phyllis Webb Fonds, 1951–1981. Library and Archives Canada LMS-0098. Referred to as "LAC."

Wilson, Edmund. "Is Verse a Dying Technique?" In *The Triple Thinkers: Ten Essays on Literature*. New York: Harcourt, Brace, 1938; revised and enlarged as *The Triple Thinkers: Twelve Essays on Literary Subjects*. New York: Oxford UP, 1948; reprinted New York: Octagon Books, 1977.

Woodcock, George. *Northern Spring: The Flowering of Canadian Literature*. Vancouver: Douglas & McIntyre, 1987.

Woolf, Virginia. *The Waves*. London: Hogarth, 1931.

Wordsworth, William. Preface to the Lyrical Ballads. In *Lyrical Ballads, with Pastoral and Other Poems*. Vol. 1, third edition. Edited by William Wordsworth. London: Longman and Rees, 1802. Republished in *The Norton Anthology of Theory and Criticism*. New York: W.W. Norton, 1986. References are to the Norton edition.

Acknowledgements

Editing Webb's *Collected Poems* has given me much pleasure and great joy. My most obvious debt of gratitude is to Phyllis Webb for having written poems in the first place, and for having agreed to let me undertake the job of editor. I also thank her for being so patient, so generous with her time and her knowledge whenever I have called upon her for help. What an extraordinary privilege to work with her as a kind of co-editor! Thanks also to Kevin Williams, publisher of Talonbooks, for giving me the opportunity to edit *Peacock Blue*, the perfect title imagined by the originator of this volume.

In addition, I wish to acknowledge the help of Linda Hoad who was the manuscripts librarian and Claude Le Moine who was the curator of the Literary Manuscripts Collection at what used to be called the National Library of Canada. For more recent help received from Catherine Hobbs, the literary manuscript archivist at what is now the Library and Archives Canada, more thanks are due. These scholars, as well as others like Ken Wilson, who prepared the 1984 "Finding Aid" to the Webb Fonds, and Cecelia Frey, who compiled the 1985 annotated bibliography on Phyllis Webb's work, have made my job so much easier.

Closer to home, my distinguished colleague Bill New saved me from public embarrassment by putting his editor's cap back on and reading the penultimate version of the introduction. For this and other acts of courage and friendship I am eternally in his debt. David Lemon, who read an earlier version of the introduction, also gave me some wise advice which I wisely took. To Smaro Kamboureli, my thanks for offering financial assistance; to Sherrill Grace, David Rampton, Bob Heidbreder, Jane Flick, and to all the members of the "Liberated Literary Ladies Society," a book-reading club of which David Farwell and I are happily Honorary Members, many thanks for the encouragement and support especially during the initial stages of editing the *Collected Poems*.

Finally, for the once-in-a-lifetime love and the nurture which keep me going, enabling me to embark on projects like this rather late in life, I thank Wayne McDermott to whom I dedicate whatever part of *Peacock Blue* can be called mine.

Trio

FIRST POEMS

FALLING GLASS
"The glass is falling hour by hour, the glass will fall forever,
But if you break the bloody glass you won't hold up the weather."

—LOUIS MACNEICE

This our inheritance
is our distress,
born of the weight of eons
it skeletons our flesh,
bearing us on
we wear it
though it bares us.

The eye's lid covers
the I aware,
the hand hovers
over, then plunders
emerging despair.

Here is our overture then
where prayers of defeat are sown –
inheritance, bright with death
spangled with bone.

POET

I am promised
I have taken the veil
I have made my obeisances
I have walked on words of nails
to knock on silences
I have tokened the veil
to my face
mouth covered with symbol
I have punctured my fingerbase
to fill one thimble
with blood for consecration
in a nunnery
I have faced each station
of the cross and to each place
have verbs tossed free, so pale
to compass the bitter male
in this changed chancellery
and I have paced four walls
of this cell, I have paced
for the word, and I have heard,
curiously, I have heard the tallest of mouths
call down behind my veil
to limit or enlarge me
as I or it prevails.

SEPTEMBER

September relishes the sharp affairs
impatient at the slow despairs
she rips up trees in her royal air

accosts the cobbled streets of loves
(old as the city, old as the dare
that made them) with her conscripted leaves,

whipping the road with seasoned gold
she flings her multicoloured cloak,
defiant, over streets that can't be closed.

THE CAMPFIRE

Erratic as unholy weather
this tent of heat commits
our hymns to fire
as we require of heat
a home, a temple.

Our breath in this warm rite
beats from the metal wish of flame
our sweet, immediate stars
debarring the statement of daylight
where hope breathes close to death.

Felt in our faith is our past
secured to our future,
these simple Quebec hills command
us communal, close-choired
in our circles, fired
by the present tense of God
we name all others foreign,
all alien, unmet by heat.

But distance dances far from the first
lessons of fire
and, tired in the collapse of morning,
suspired as the untempled We,
our spectacular tent crashes,
surrenders only a black circle
on dead ground
and the disappointment of ashes.

THE SKYWRITER

The plane writes love large
 across our sky
  white as light
   as round as blown
    as the proverbial
     cloud fleecy
      as swiftly gone.

I should have known
 long before the winter fell
  unretractable
   into the overcoat's
    parochial shell
     that spring meant
      something ephemeral
       as this air-fancier's wit
        sketching in the sky
         of your epithet.

The slight touch
 and the words turn
  (the spelling of swift eyes)
   higher he lifts
    as lightly signifies
     the cloud's wind over
      demise of lover.

THE COLOUR OF THE LIGHT

I.

On the apparent corner of two streets
a strange man shook
a blue cape above my head,
I saw it as the shaking sky
and was forthwith ravished.

II.

A man bent to light a cigarette.
This was in the park
and I was passing through.
With what succinct ease he joins
himself to flame!
I passed by silently noting
how clear were the colours of pigeons
and how mysterious the animation of children
playing in trees.

III.

When a strange man arrays
a dispassionate quality before
his public, the public may be deceived,
but a man's strange passion
thrusts deeper and deeper
into its fire of dispassionate
hard red gems.

IV.

And the self is a grave
music will not mould
nor grief destroy:
yet this does not make refusal:
somehow ... somehow ...
shapes fall in a torrent of design
and over the violent space
assume a convention;

or in the white, white quivering
instability of love
we shake a world to order:
our prismed eyes divide such light
as this world dreams on
and rarely sees.

I thought I saw the pigeons in the trees ...

CHUNG YUNG

The year has come round full circle,
all evidence, both external and internal,
is now proven and visible;

love has known all seasons, cycles within cycles have
given birth
to words, patterns, moods
and placed their worth
in necessary violence
or in absolution.

Purchases have been made
wisely or imprudently
neither all being lost
nor all gained;

balance, delicate
yet fibred,
proves a pivot
around which are described
immaculate arcs.

"The word *chung* signifies what is bent neither to one side
nor to the other. The word *yung* signifies unchanging.
What exists plumb in the middle is the just process of the
universe and that which never wavers or wobbles is the
calm principle in its mode of action."

TO ......

The spring's vivid fingers
untwine no memories
and birds, moons, possible songs
and eyes deal only death
to the suns and hands
of my gestures.
It is only you, when
you stroke my wrist with your whisper,
who can round my life ring
the uncustomary blossoms
that rhyme with my singular spring.

INTROSPECTIVE LOVERS

They quiet lie.
Both in silent
and singular pursuit of thought
while the beauty of them each
to each is quite disclosed
through quiet touch of eye.
The words slip into gold unuttered,
and words slip into gold!
Seduced is sophistical thought,
stripped, and is known;
sensed is the green, grape pulse,
caught, and is torn.
Word and the gold are grape, and the eye undone,
green and the pulse are word, and the heart unstrung.

THE SECOND HAND

Here, Love, whether we love or not
involves the clock and its ignorant hands
tying our hearts in a lover's knot;

now, whether we flower or not
requires a reluctance in the hour;
yet we cannot move, in the present caught

in the embrace of to be or not;
dear, shall we move our hands together,
or must we bear the onslaught

of the tick, the tock, the icy draught
of a clock's arms swinging themselves together –
or now shall we kiss where once we laughed?

all time is sadness but the heart is not
unmoved in the minute of the dancing measure,
for if in the pressing stress of time

the dancer stays, or act is mime,
hands must break by being caught
as the clock covers its face with an evil weather.

EARTH DESCENDING

"This is the end," she said
and flapped from the room,
"This is the plan," she said
and twirled from the moon's
spooning and kissing and,
swishing, she fled the armorial night
and quietly said,
"I am free from the sun's orbit
and morbid regulated glances daily,
and free also from the moon's nightly
slightly sickening romances
and erased is oracular Mars and satyred Saturn
along with Pluto and the rest
of the nocturnal floral pattern.

"Now I am nothing but a spat star
and I like this high-tailing it to hell
and almost swell it is to kick up
blue dust atmospheric
(especially when one is used to
regulated black and white dust cleric).
For me right now
(and this is the end right now)
I am pleased with these planispheric reelings
and if I were more the pig and less the planet
well, yes, dammit,
I'd squeal that this cannot, cannot
be as good as it seems
to be freed from old Electra
(and even Oedipus)
who have always hovered
and in all and every emergency
lowered the lid over the eye and me
covered with night,
(polite name for lack of sight
and of what Milton most complained)
wound me up and set me saying,
        'the end is not yet'
        'the end is not yet'

O, if they could only know
that at this moment as I splutter
and now and then twirl and flutter
into a space downward
      'upon my word!'
quadrupled, and then again
would it be said.
O, how I would love
to bet the dear old couple
the salacious solar system
against seven buckets of the Milky Way
that this earthy eye
(it is I)
rowing wildly away
from some universal dock
with a leap in my heart which amounts
to a tick-tock clocked bomb inside me
houred for that existential arm
of the witch below
whose ripe, black brew,
smouldering and mouldering
with happy spat stars
is eager to receive another.

"For I, like others,
have slipped over the solar edge
spat and said,
'This is the end,
to hell with that eternal circulation
of night, day, life, death and love all over,
this is the end of an earth well worn
and born to die
and so say I
this is the end.
No need to belabour the point, however,
This is the end – and right now, moreover.' "

PINING

Sense of loss
across
my hand –
it droops
to my side –
I stand
wilting
like some poor
summer flower
of tradition –
something less than
tragic, an act,
a mimic of the great,
the giant crack
in the spine,
the central agony.

What I need
is a cosmic break
and not this
meddlesome
distortion
of the
fact.

LEAR ON THE BEACH AT BREAK OF DAY

Down on the beach at break of day
observe Lear calmly observing the sea:
he tosses the buttons of his sanity
like aged pebbles into the bay;

cold, as his sexless daughters were,
the pebbles are round by a joyless war,
worn down on a troubled, courtly ground,
they drop in the sea without a sound;

and the sea repeats their logical sin,
shedding ring after ring of watery thin
wheels of misfortune of crises shorn
which spin to no end – and never turn.

And there Lear stands, alone.
The sun is rising and the cliffs aspire,
and there Lear stands, with dark small stones
in his crazed old hands. But farther and higher

he hurls them now, as if to free
himself with them. But only stones drop
sullenly, a hardened crop,
into the soft, irrational sea.

ELEGY ON THE DEATH OF DYLAN THOMAS

Dylan is dead
of a round sun,
heart and brain
spun round in one.

Dylan is dead
the ivy's curled
dead on its stalk,
its dread furled.

Dylan is dead.
In the winded rain
I heard his son
in Dylan's pain:

Gold was my father,
green was his will
which swung out farther
than broken hills,

than his poems said.
Dylan is dead.
But Death's gone gold
down one honeyed night;

yet, we have cried,
Dylan has died,
bold and old
in the mercy of his blight;

an impatient moth cajoled
breaks from the apple of our sight.

THE CONSTRUCT OF YEARS

Aeschylus, a tragic dramatist,
525–456 BC,
serves sufficiently to indicate
the going downwards of the dates
before Christ:

with Christ
the years achieved a zero;
after him, they crept along
the upward accidents of heroes
in time's accumulation:

pause, then, contemporary,
in Elizabeth's long face,
1558–1603 AD,
gaze in her cold round eyes

see circles of wonder whose pupils of faith
have hardened stiff to curse and rhyme
the cruel, articulate
compassing of time.

STANDING

for Earle Birney

Up from all fours,
                          crawling through slime
to aspects of the dry
human condition,

upward
          from the knees erect, shouldered,
midget,
          of many created things one of the few
                          that can blush
                                        and stand on its own two

feet.   Found
                          standing in theatre crowds
          and in queues
for meat.

Yes
      we can stand
                          strutting a met-
aphor. We stand and we
stand, can please each

other
          with chat at cocktail parties,
make speech,
          array sufficient surety,
                          play with words
                                        here is our pride, the stride of

tongue, sends
                          leaping in public view
          our syllables
of lung.

"Yes,
          the soldier, for
                          treason, was shot

standing against the wall –
yes, if I recall,

he was
        like any other soldier
badged
        in regimental discipline, excellent
                in coordination
                        gallant in disposition

towards
        giving and receiving respect,
    and in all
correct:

eyes
        front, shoulders
                        back, head high, held
himself above himself
he died finally

against a wall." Caught in thought the Pro-
fessor
        in the dim hallway stands calling
                the classic stars.
                        Flights of the mind from the

earth are sure.
                Peripatetics knew
        the value of
posture:

head
        up, head down?
                        At any rate
standing on two sound legs
and circulating.

"Thanks
      lady, but if I can just get
a-hold
      of this pole I can stand all right."
          Poor cripple –
               knows the irrelevance of
defeat? No,
        for custom still controls
   (at times)
the feet:

stand
    up when ladies
             enter the room;
to let the drunkard pass
draw aside

in awe
    for the princess bowing from
her Rolls
      or the president from his Cadillac.
        Lovers are known
           at first to stand, then face

the fact: love,
        deliberate regression;
   futurity
is tact;

like
   illness, when
           to lie down
is a kind of taking
of a crown.

The king
          is dead, long live the king. Re-
volving
          the bright rock turns, arrival and de-
                    parture, depositing
                              silver, night after

day: child
          of derivative face – "the
     moon is up"
we say

up,
     and we command
                              image be man
and aspect of the wry
human condition;

or any
          day in front of a painting stand,
discern
          "objective correlative." And stance is ours,
                    artists' and everyman's
                              our distinguished visitor

to be handled
          with care. Care, one aspect only
     of our freedom –
enlightening

as learning to walk.

TO A ZEN BUDDHIST WHO LAUGHS DAILY

Oh laugh, laugh out the butterflies and dragons
from the places of desire,
roar out the dalliance of the poppy's core,
laugh out the lotus and hang it on
pools of intuition.

Oh chant, chant out the intellect, blaspheme
our sacred jungle mind,
sing out the answers from the holy shrine
of Nowhere, shuffle the plume
of Emptiness and scream

oh scream in furious daily rite,
release the throttles of the monkish fires,
pacify all thought in reeling roars,
laugh out this question: the goose is tight
in a bottle,

how to release without injury?
The answer is plain: "There, it's out!"
Oh shout, scream, volley
the soul with laughing dreams of light,

dragons are scuttled down laughter's lane,
and scorched butterflies fall
in the achievement of Light.

Zen is said to be the only religion in which laughter is part of the priestly
ritual. Zen techniques to achieve Enlightenment (Satori) are various,
often quaint, often intensely sane. The rapid question-and-answer
method between master and novice is one of many in which insights
are gained; to go beyond the intellect is essential: "Zen roars with
laughter at reasoning, logic and the laws of thought."

PAIN

Whether pain is simple as razors edging the fleshy cage,
or whether pain raves with shark inside the ribs,
it throws a bridge of value to belief
where, towards or away from, moves intense traffic.

Or, should the eyes focus to cubes and lights of pain
and the breasts' exquisite asterisks breed circular grief,
this bird of death is radiant and complex,
speeds fractional life over value to belief;

the bridge spans by contemporary pain
centuries of historical birth.

AND IN OUR TIME

A world flew in my mouth with our first kiss
and its wings were dipped in all the flavours of grief.
Oh my darling, tell me, what can love mean in such a world,
and what can we or any lovers hold in this immensity
of hate and broken things?
Now it is down, down, that's where your kiss travels me,
and, as a world tumbling shocks the theories of spheres,
so this love is like falling glass shaking with stars
the air which tomorrow, or even today, will be
a slow, terrible movement of scars.

PATIENCE

Patience is the wideness of the night
the simple pain of stars
the muffled explosion of velvet
it moves itself generally
through particulars
accepts the telling of time
without day's relativity.

But more than these accommodations
patience is love withdrawn
into the well; immersion into
a deep place where green begins.
It is the slow beat of slanting eyes
down the heart's years,
it is the silencer
and the loving now
involves no word.
Patience is the answer
poised in grief – the knowing –
it is the prose of tears
withheld and the aging,
the history in the heart
and futures where pain
is a lucid cargo.

Even Your Right Eye

for D'O

You cannot take all luggage with you
on all journeys; on one journey even your
right hand and your right eye may be
among the things you have to leave behind.

—C.S. LEWIS

I

THE MIND READER

I thought,
and he acted
upon my thought,
read by some wonderful
kind of glass my mind
saw passing that way
gulls floating over boats
floating in the bay,
and by some wonderful
sleight of hand
he ordered the gulls to land
on boats
and the boats to land.

Or, was it through waves
he sent the boats
to fly with gulls
so that out of care
they all could play
in a wonderful
gull-boat-water way
up in a land of air?

FRAGMENT

That violet
   either in the grove
      or in the light

is the minute particle
      of an area's given growth;

Speak to that violet
     or to the light

and what is given back
       is not echo
but the mute substance
      of the work of love.

MARVELL'S GARDEN

Marvell's garden, that place of solitude,
is not where I'd choose to live
yet is the fixed sundial
that turns me round
unwillingly
in a hot glade
as closer, closer I come to contradiction
to the shade green within the green shade.

The garden where Marvell scorned love's solicitude –
that dream – and played instead an arcane solitaire,
shuffling his thoughts like shadowy chance
across the shrubs of ecstasy,
and cast the myths away to flowering hours
as yes, his mind, that sea, caught at green
thoughts shadowing a green infinity.

And yet Marvell's garden was not Plato's
garden – and yet – he did care more for the form
of things than for the thing itself –
ideas and visions,
resemblances and echoes,
things seeming and being
not quite what they were.

That was his garden, a kind of attitude
struck out of an earth too carefully attended,
wanting to be left alone.
And I don't blame him for that.
God knows, too many fences fence us out
and his garden closed in on Paradise.

On Paradise! When I think of his hymning
Puritans in the Bermudas, the bright oranges
lighting up that night! When I recall
his rustling tinsel hopes
beneath the cold decree of steel,
Oh, I have wept for some new convulsion
to tear together this world and his.

But then I saw his luminous plumed Wings
prepared for flight,
and then I heard him singing glory
in a green tree,
and then I caught the vest he'd laid aside
all blest with fire.

And I have gone walking slowly in
his garden of necessity
leaving brothers, lovers, Christ
outside my walls
where they have wept without
and I within.

MARIAN SCOTT

If she is a moth
then all light is lured toward her,
this she consumes and becomes
the moth burning in its own light.
Brighter than all the stars and planets
her central flame transmutes
the nerveless sun into a spine of white
which darts the imageless world back into space.
Pigments she takes and breaks them into one
pearl smoking whiteness, and then eye
directs hand to flourish the first morning
into fire. The walls float from her house
and wing with paintings into all ourselves
for I have seen around her head flying
the whole career of colour,
and in her hands the age of darkness dying.
Light, oh it swims from the tragic sun
into her instant miracle
where, caught in the wire net of form,
she twists and turns it into day's
urchins and angels –
blood of our blood, bone of her luminous bone.

SPROUTS THE BITTER GRAIN

Sprouts the bitter grain in my heart,
green and fervent it grows as all
this lush summer rises in heats about me,
calls along the vines of my wrath,
chokes and enchants my eyes.
Even the crows that nest in this valvular forest
scream and collect the glittering fires
of my hatreds, dispose this desperate love,
my fury, amid the sinister leaves.
Hot, the wind threatens my trees with weather,
rushes the crows to skies of their ancient glory,
vultures, and I watch, tormented by sun.
I am all land to this malignant grain, ambiguous,
it burgeons in a single season, like fear.
Like fear I have known it, a forest of green angels,
a threat of magnificent beasts. And Oh, I call,
Oh, to the gods of the temperate climes,
Praise me, destroy these criminal branches,
bring me – soft – the weather of meadows,
the seasons and gardens of children.

SACRAMENT OF SPRING

Spring, with a laying on of hands,
strips me of flesh and leaves me living,
flays with a wish of all the fevers,
burns me with every flower's brand;

for I have left my love forever,
but I have locked his bones in me.

Spring, expounding this Day of Judgment,
scorns the year with the central sun,
explores the air with pearls of wisdom,
invests the living buds with scent.

But I have left my love forever,
and I have locked his bones in me.

Grafting the living and the dead
into the flesh of eternity,
spring requires of the present dread
now must the I become the We.

I have left my love forever.
I have locked his bones in me.

Spring, holding the whip in acts of love,
a stern master with too many tasks,
the bones are cracking in the dove,
yet the architecture cannot ask,

nor cry, and cannot fall.
The corpse is moving in the spring.
Only the living know the dead.
The flower and the whip are wed.

And I have left my love forever.
Slowly, his bones are moving me.

A WALK BY THE SEINE

This water flowing
down through a clutch of stones,
this bank we walk along,
and old river-men fishing
toss song in a net of motion
that draws our joined hands
too close to the edge.

This river towing
barges, suicides, small fish, its own
miraculous currents, and the strong
cities of peace and war, all washing
down to an ominous ocean
where even our looping thoughts are fanned
across a sea of knowledge.

These leaning, bearded, dark men knowing
ultimate tragedy moans
like a siren down from the long
sky, cover their eyes, wishing,
wishing they had not seen our devotion
to the straight course in a crooked land
and our final pledge.

But you and I slowing
our words to a muted tone
(for beauty silences the horse-drawn
carriages of wisdom), meshing
light and leaves in that imperial notion
of stasis and dream, move and stand,
like love and death, at the river's edge.

THE SHAPE OF PRAYER

The shape of prayer
is like the shape of the small
beach stone, rounded smooth, but individual
in its despair,
skimmed on the water it skips to drown
down with its sunken fellows, down
in despair.
The shape of prayer is that –
curved and going nowhere, to fall
in pure abstraction saying everything
and saying nothing at all.

CURTAINS

An artist worked on these
somewhere behind the print, the texture
and the tint, and scattered leaves
across a golden ground where they fell down
as simply as they fell, and left abstractions
curving in my breeze. The lunchtime sun discovers
butterflies and loops them through autumnal dells
of aspen, elm, maple and alder leaves
down to this grove where only sun is mover,
where I am moved by pure design, feel,
and October colour – abstractly drowned in autumn sun
smothered in leaves and leafmould smells.
Thus I elaborate a rite
and draw the curtains on a summer's sigh
haul in these dying coloured kites
call in the leafless winter that I shun.

FANTASIA ON CHRISTIAN'S DIARY

There have been no animals
except snowflakes falling,
the whites of our eyes falling,
the white skies, our sides falling,
the flesh made air, and the air made bone.

> *When will the caribou come?*
> *When will the caribou come?*

What has Jack Hornby come for?
Not to stake claims –
he explores only
mineral silence to enter the
initials of the name.

> *When will the caribou come –*
> *I don't mean to stay –*
> *But when will they come?*

Oh, but they did come! They strode
to our house, bitter and lean,
and then fled away.
But we were away, and should perhaps
have gone on forever, or never
have come at all,
now that we find so many white deaths
want to call.

But don't blame Jack.
He lays a foundation
I can build my life on.
(Christian dying at eighteen
disease in his back,
knees sharp as antlers.)
It was just that we didn't prepare.
We eat everything to the bone.

> *When will the caribou come?*
> *When will they come.*

It is cold, fifty below, and the silence
is louder than light,
Jack's heart weakens, we sicken,
and the mind is ice.

Oh, when will they come!

The calcium nights shudder to powder
– everything is white! Up there
the swans are flakes, the skies are
falling down,
yet for all the natural effort
nothing but white is shown,
Certainly, there are nights one dare not sleep.
Our scattered lawns are deathly white with sheep,
and all our speckled hopes on fawn's feet pass.

Now tracks we left I've gathered for the stove
to seal up tight a trinity of love
as unexplained, as unreleased as night.
All the wills that ever were will burn
and end in ashes when we die.
The trails of our exploration
passed us by.

But when will the caribou come?
When will they come to eat from my hand?

The sky roars down with animals.
Don't look! Don't look!
There must be a million reindeer
solid as land!

This poem, inspired by the CBC documentary "Death in the Barren Grounds" by George Whalley, does not tell the story set forth in Edgar Christian's diary of the tragic exploration in the Subarctic Barrens, which the broadcast did so admirably. It attempts rather to give a shade to the atmosphere of that story, often by using quotations, both of fact and word, and even at times of fancy. Edgar Christian was seventeen when he came to Canada in 1926 with his uncle, Jack Hornby, to make a trek to the Barren Grounds. There was a third member of the team, Harold Adlard. They failed to put in sufficient supplies and all died, first Jack, then Harold, and finally Edgar. Christian, before he died, placed his diary, letters, and the will in the stove, presumably for safekeeping. Hornby, a remarkable man and an explorer of unique intention, had started a book and this was placed in a suitcase. The hut was discovered and reported in 1928, but it was not until 1929, when the RCMP reached the cabin, that the skeletons were found, and the papers, and this Arctic's *Pilgrim's Progress* of the 1920s was unfolded.

LAMENT

Knowing that everything is wrong,
how can we go on giving birth
either to poems or the troublesome lie,
to children, most of all, who sense
the stress in our distracted wonder
the instant of their entry with their cry?

For every building in this world
receives our benediction of disease.
Knowing that everything is wrong
means only that we all know where we're going.

But I, how can I, I,
craving the resolution of my earth,
take up my little gang of sweet pretence
and saunter day-dreary down the alleys, or pursue
the half-disastrous night? Where is that virtue
I would claim with tense impersonal unworth,
where does it dwell, that virtuous land
where one can die without a second birth?

It is not here, neither in the petulance
of my cries, nor in the tracers of my active fear,
not in my suicide of love, my dear.
That place of perfect animals and men
is simply the circle we would charm our children in
and why we frame our lonely poems in
the shape of a frugal sadness.

II

MOMENTS ARE MONUMENTS

moments are monuments
   if caught
      carved into stone

caught
   pressed into words
      made crazy in colour

made act
   as in love
      made debt
         as in deed

that deed
   done well
      towering
         done ill

no one knows better
   the zones of time
      than active man
         frustrate in history

captured in glass
   seen through like a lens
      refracted in space

no one knows better
   no one knows
      the sad process of building

out of broken time
   eras from heart's beat
      out of broken space
         arches from heart's break

OLD WOMAN

Her skin has dried and wrinkled
like a continent,
like a continent
without motion and only one season
where everything is repeated that has been said.

Her heart has dried and shrivelled
into a small ruin,
into a small ruin
her life crumbles, and only one cause –
people dying everywhere, repeating her dread.

Her hands have dried and withered
into white claws,
into white claws
with nothing to clutch, only her fear
that sleeps at her throat like her ghostly beloved.

Her eyes have failed as life failed
like dying stars,
like dying stars
her night darkens and only refers
her dyingness to darkness and a hard god.

MOURNING BALLAD

He came to me in mourning clothes
on the day after Christmas,
oh he came to me in the morning
to bring me his gift of kisses.

So he took off his funeral greatcoat
and removed his funereal tie,
and we laughed at his gentleman's silksocks
as he tossed them up so high

they fell on top of his darksuit
left on the corner chair,
and we loved in the crossed hours of mourning
to make our funeral fair.

RHETORIC FOR NEW YEARS

Above the necessary tragedy of a sharp world
where the standing gods can only wound and wait,
the dark songs of tortured harps
resound against the echo of an age.

And if you ask me through the splintering day
whether the doom has come
or is that Second Coming,
strangers on an island like a stage

make muted signs as for the deaf and dumb
and, pointing to the tide, mime out
the sea, its coming in and going out.
And if you ask me (and who are you and who am I?)

whether the doom is worth an anguished night,
I'll slip the moon down from the moneyed sky
and flip it on the chance of answering light,
a bet that once devised cannot be won

for around that moon hovered the fathering sun,
for all that travels is as circular
and all that loves is as an endless rage
about a world that harbours griefs like gifts
then casts them trinket-like across the stage
that shifts like an island in the sea, uneasily,
like the age.

DOUBLE ENTENDRE

The seed white
            beneath the flesh
                        red and diamonded
                                    under the skin
                                                rough, round,

of the round pomegranate
                        hopes in essential shape
                                    for a constellation of fruit

just as the pregnant woman
                        in the street
                                    carrying her three-year-old son

is one and entire
                        the tribe of woman
                                    weighed down by the race of man –
                                                always to be renewed,

for the man killed
                        by the Temple clock when it fell
                                    told me time had not stopped –
                                                or only for him

                                    though I saw

in this unflattering
                        accidental
                                    irony
                                                that he had indeed come

to a timely end
                        within the courtyards of the English
                                    Courts of Law.

And by these exaggerations of the
                        nature of the Thing

(Octavian dressed up as a boy
                    dressed up as a girl
                              in *Der Rosenkavalier*,
the portrait of the artist
                    holding a mirror,

or Gide
          in his *Journals*
                    writing of Stendhal's)

we come to a heightened fancy
                    and a tightened fact:

the fact that man must
                    make, make

                              bone, flesh,

a structure for his loss

          and, like gold, take
                    seeds of meaning

                    pitiful

          from the dross.

For in his strange
                    peripheral orbit
                              of reality and dream

he wanders, wonders,
                    through the play within the play

                              knowing not

                                        which is the right

                                        the light

the star in the cold, staring sky,

          or the star reflected in a human eye?

TWO VERSIONS

I. POETRY

Fidelity
          as in love
                    is in poetry
                              an unexpected satisfaction;

or, rendered into French,
          The Importance of Being Earnest becomes
L'important, c'est d'être fidèle !

discoverable after promiscuities,
                    flirtations,
                              flights of fancy;

this is to say that
          genius is no scarecrow,
     for instance:
                    murder in South Kensington
is not strange fruit on any poet's tree;

     for instance:
                    the hoodwinked eye of ignorance
lurks sinister beneath the professorial gown;

or,
     extremes of possibility are not always
          the greatest possible extremities,

               for,
                    like a monk in meditation,

poetry
          is cloaked in sheer
                    profundities of otherness,

its ambiguous nakedness, its serene capacity
                    for wisdom: nothing denied

until entirely known.

And so, in the chaste embrace
of faithful lovers
poetry may
freely ravage the pulse of evil
that throbs in the dark incestuous part
of every earnest lover's earthly heart.

II. IN SITU

The poet in his tree of hell
will see life steadily and see it well.

The world is round.   It moves in circles.

The poet in his vision tree
imparts immaculate necessity
to murder, ignorance and lust.

The world is round.   It moves in circles.

Poetry, the poet's curse,
will look for better or for worse
like a simple monk in meditation

cloaked in apparent deprivation:
in its ambiguous nakedness
glows the raiment of its otherness.

The world is round.   It moves in circles.

With laughter on his haunted face,
a madman captive in a leaf's embrace,
the poet wildly shakes his tree.

The world is round.   It moves in circles.

INCIDENTAL

In that indelible year
when the soldiers came
and the dogs and harpies visited churches
the creatures of my infant dreams
rose up in agony and fear
and splayed the air with foetal screams
and left the year uncompromised.

The year then knew its form and fled
into the cities of the dead.

RUST ON AN ANCHOR

If to be remote
       (if only momentarily)
        as a Chinese poem

is to achieve sanity

then you and I
       like a Japanese ballet
        touch it as if

between the acts
       of a violent comedy
        a way to say

now and then
       the rare mountain air
        is caught
          in a small

Venetian glass bottle
       (used for a time

in early eighteenth-century England

       for snuff for the

pleasure of sneezing

        a mild and conscious apoplexy).

SUNDAY MORNING WALK

Brisker than the answer to
                Two and Two
                                (makes Four!)

my Sunday morning walk
                (on which I pick up *The Observer*
                                for threepence halfpenny)
takes me to several answers
                and no conclusions.

Around the park
                past the Round Pond
                                where children sail boats
                                                and swans sail,

I go in search
                neither intense nor anxious
                but in observation of the small event:

the brown dog winding after the wind,
                the chestnut in the moist autumn leaves,
                                an old man flying kites on the heath.

These
        events
                these separate
                        minutiae
                                dot the horizon
                                        like

small birds flying south for winter
        leaving quick facts
                in my collection of unknowns,

making the new familiar,
                and now intense.
                        Vitality
                          brisk
                           cold

assertion
        like dawn
                not to be taken lightly.
                        Perhaps some day
                            to be taken back

to you.

1962

The Sea Is Also a Garden

for my mothers
Mary Webb
and Lucy Jones

But the sea
which no one tends
is also a garden

—WILLIAM CARLOS WILLIAMS

Mad gardener to the sea, the moon

    rages across the sky to tend

        oceans of an unloving dark

            and the bone-blooming skeleton:

beyond all Paradise, all Arden

    moon multiplies the garden;

        nor doth the coral orchard care

            man dreameth ever back to water –

l'homme inconnu et solitaire.

PROPOSITIONS

I could divide a leaf
and give you half.

Or I could search for two leaves
sending you one.

Or I could walk to the river
and look across

and seeing you there,
or not there,

absence or presence,
would spring the balance to my day.

Or I could directly find you and take your hand
so that one hand would be given

and one kept, like a split leaf
or like two leaves separate.

These would be signs and offerings:
the just passion, just encountering.

Or we perhaps could speed four eyes,
the chariot horses of our dreams and visions,

in them direction and decision find.
The split leaf floating on the river,

the hand sketching in the air
a half-moon, its hidden wholeness there.

COUNTERED

An easy climate with all the elements,
earth, air, fire, water.
A desperate system solid as it is human.
Dust is falling where dust has climbed.
The sun is patient, moon calm,
the sin of knowledge almost innocence.
Love has become goodwill, as grief has,
as torturing strength has warped to sanity.
Now dustbowl earth completes its nothingness,
every bright image, lark or cardinal,
has dropped its wings, has moulted in disgust.
The lucid mind fumbles to doors and falls.
The crusted eyes tears cannot clarify.
But traveller dust which notices our earth
we totally invite until we die.
Now earth must spin as little as it is
as it has spun before our vast illusion.
Now loves will tumble on dark beds of space.
Loves will tumble now in any case.
But eyes of power, the long mileage to stars
our sleep will dreaden and intensify.
Lovers will love, and all the instant world
will tether joy, creation's sweet pathetic trust,
while our participating marrow
clicks with destroying dust.

BREAKING

Give us wholeness, for we are broken.
But who are we asking, and why do we ask?
Destructive element heaves close to home,
our years of work broken against a breakwater.

Shattered gods, self-iconoclasts,
it is with Lazarus unattended we belong
(the fall of the sparrow is unbroken song).
The crucifix has clattered to the ground,
the living Christ has spent a year in Paris,
travelled on the Metro, fallen in the Seine.
We would not raise our silly gods again.
Stigmata sting, they suddenly appear
on every blessed person everywhere.
If there is agitation there is cause.

Ophelia, Hamlet, Othello, Lear,
Kit Smart, William Blake, John Clare,
Van Gogh, Henry IV of Pirandello,
Gérard de Nerval, Antonin Artaud
bear a crown of darkness.
It is better so.

Responsible now each to his own attack,
we are bequeathed their ethos and our death.
Greek marble white and whiter grows
breaking into history of a west.
If we could stand so virtuously white
crumbling in the terrible Grecian light.

There is a justice in destruction.
It isn't "isn't fair."
A madhouse is designed for the insane,
a hospital for wounds that will reopen;
a war is architecture for aggression,
and Christ's stigmata body-minted token.
What are we whole or beautiful or good for
but to be absolutely broken?

MAKING

Quilted
patches, unlike the smooth silk loveliness
of the bought,
this made-ness out of self-madness
thrown across their bones to keep them warm.
It does.

Making
under the patches a smooth silk loveliness
of parts:
two bodies are better than one for this quilting,
throwing into the dark a this-ness that was not.
It does.

Fragments
of the splintered irrelevance of doubt, sharp
hopes, spear and splice into a nice consistency as once
under the pen, the brush, the sculptor's hand
music was made, arises now, blossom on fruit-tree bough.
It does.

Exercise,
exegesis of the will captures and lays
haloes around bright ankles of a saint.
Exemplary under the tree,
Buddha glows out now
making the intolerable, accidental sky
patch up its fugitive ecstasies.
It does.

It does,
and, all doing done, a child on the street runs
dirty from sun
to the warm infant born to soiled sheets
and stares at the patched external face.
It does.

From the making made and, made, now making
certain order – thus excellent despair
is laid, and in the room the patches of the quilt
seize light and throw it back upon the air.
A grace is made, a loveliness is caught
quilting a quiet blossom as a work.
It does.

And do you,
doubting, fractured, and untaught, St. John of the Cross,
come down and patch the particles and throw
across the mild unblessedness of day
lectures to the untranscended soul.
Then lotus-like you'll move upon the pond,
the one-in-many, the many-in-the-one,
making a numbered floral-essenced sun
resting upon the greening padded frond,
a patched, matched protection for Because,
And for our dubious value it will do.
It always does.

BOMB SHELTER

Nakedness is our shelter.
Bones are only temporal.
Yes, there will be splinters.
Yes, there will be cancers
to split this partial temple.

But, like St. Sebastian,
in love with our destruction,
at least await deliverance
from a familiar essence.
Flesh, sheltering all within,
bodied forth the architect,
nor will he go till he deploys
skin's widowed, gross philosophies.

There will be a sign
in this quick conundrum.
As arrows pierce the liver
Prometheus moves in the mirror
the eagle soars toward the chemic sun
till saint and man and god are done.
There were no chains.
There are no chains to come.

But more than wait in shining skin
with undeveloped gill and fin
we must swim dark in phosphorous seas
with whales and rayfish and amoeba
with the spinning aqueous plethora
taste the faults salting down the tide
and in our nakedness
and in our peace abide.

"THE TIME OF MAN"
extrapolations from an article by Dr. Loren Eiseley

"The little toe is attractive

                  to the student of rudimentary
and vanishing organs,"

and whooping cranes claxon

                    to the spellbound preservers
of what would naturally vanish.

When the adored ones

                pass through the door ("the future
of no invention can be guaranteed")

who does not follow them,

                half in love with his tears,
tickled by the lower brain,
            "the fossil remnant,"
                    claws

        scratching at the large
              symbolic order,
animal sad, watching the members
                fade:

        clitoral love, the royal we
              stumbling:
"The perfectly adjusted perish with their environment"

      – then take me with you
            crying
              take me with you –

The brain when it began to grow

            was "shielded by a shell of bone
as thick as a warrior's helmet."

TWO PEARS: A STILL LIFE

Two pears
   a slight distance over there
      unmoving within the golden

time-globe
   not by wind swung
      nor from branch suspended

but plucked
   now placed before the eyes'
      encountering where sudden love

returns
   all prodigal from arid outlands
      scrub, cactus, anguish of being.

The pears
   fruit, the first idea, seed
      into core into pulp and glowing

skin, love's
   radical contour shines here in stillness
      secret, original, a dream of candor.

THREE HAIKU ON A LITERARY THEME

I.

"A garden inclosed
is my sister, my spouse." Bloom
blue delphinium.

II.

Gardener is will,
"Our bodies are our gardens."
Insect, who are you?

III.

Heart's flowering. "A
garden is a lovesome thing,"
December lover.

IMAGES IN CRYSTAL

Crystal cuts sharp again into the mind
as love came clear that once-upon-a-time,
so crystal takes this morning and this air,
dazzles the shadow, the sentiment, and finds
diamond calligraphy, crystalized despairs.

Venetian workers blowing that glass horse
which catches now the Paris atmosphere,
that chandelier upholding one friend's doom
reflected in the mirrors of his room;
and then the crystal slipping through the night
as Coleridge noted moonlight stops a tear;
only this burning crystal at the heart
cuts into time and daggers into near
slaying flesh, here crystal cannot come
and live endeared. Here crystal mortifies the flesh
as love withdraws inside its crystal tomb.

A thousand chandeliers flare up, a glass horse
trots through light and splinters into ruin.

GALAXY

A curious bright tragedy grew that week
as if a luminous chandelier
had hung and swung a hundred years
but suddenly burst to a throng of stars
taking the night into a system total, luminous,
oracular, creating, catching, describing
my long love and my long waiting.
All the glass of my tears and motion
of my desires hung there in the night sky
and this was the shape of my loving,
a crystal fire flung from the great-globe moon,
sun, universe, shaking there, shining,
and deep distances dark, around and around,
and loneliness there complete and in the night
shining, shining.

THE GLASS CASTLE

The glass castle is my image for the mind
that if outmoded has its public beauty.
It can contain both talisman and leaf,
private action, homely disbelief.
And I have lived there as you must
and scratched with diamond and gathered diamond dust,
have signed the castle's tense and fragile glass
and heard the antique whores and stoned Cassandras
call me, and I answered in the one voice I knew,
"I am here. I do not know ..."
but moved the symbols and polished up the view.
For who can refrain, from action –
there is always a princely kiss for the Sleeping Beauty –
when even to put out the light takes a steady hand,
for the reward of darkness in a glass castle
is starry and full of glory.

I do not mean I shall not crack the pane.
I merely make a statement, judicious and polite,
that in this poise of crystal space
I balance and I claim the five gods of reality
to bless and keep me sane.

LOVE STORY

It was easy to see what he was up to,
the grey, bundled ape,
as he sidled half-playfully
up to the baby
and with a sly look behind
put his hands onto the crib
and leapt in.

The child's pink, beginning face
stared up as the hair-handed monkey
explored the flesh, so soft, of our infant race.
The belly spread like plush to the monkey's haunch,
he settled, heavy and gay, his nuzzling
mouth at the baby's neck.

But, no answer accurate to a smile,
he bit, tasted time, maddened,
and his nails rooted sudden fire in the ribs of Adam,
towered, carnivorous, for aim
and baby face, ears, arms
were torn and taken in his ravaging.

And so the killing, too-late parents came,
hysteric, after their child's
futile pulse had stopped its beating.
Only the half-pathetic, half-triumphant
monkey peered out from the crib,
bobbed nervously on the dead infant's belly,
then stopped, suddenly paralyzed on that soft tomb.

Was it the donkey death brayed out at him
from the human mother's eyes,
or did his love for her in that pause
consume him?

The jealous ape's death was swift
and of natural cause. "Died of shame,"
some said, others, "of shock."
But his death was Othello's death,
as great, as picayune,
he died of envy, lacking the knack of wisdom.

PLANKTON NOR PERCH ...

Plankton nor perch
in this sea,
no salmon silvering
this lost lagoon,
only the heron fishing
for a fin or two
and a gull moored on the wind.

In arcs and crises
wings out this love
to no sea, but see
the birds of the eyes
are plumed in fire
feathering the elements of desire
but do not catch the splitting
at the marrow.

Your hands and the bones
of your bastioned heart
fever my winter,
breath burns in the air,
and I offer only time,
the splintering fingers I own,
the birds of my eyes
and brevity of bone.

BEACHCOMBER

Because she insists on waking nightmares,
I'm thrown out of bed in just the way
old man night is tossed out by day.
What is there left for a faded star?
I escape to the beach at seven thirty
and alarm the others who arrived before
to stare at the mountains or cry on the shore.

The beach cleaner combs the leftovers
of burnt-up yesterday's savage sunbathers –
those are eyes that were her pearls –
he rakes his briny treasury –
Hey! Leave something for me!
All he leaves is sand and stone,
but the sea and mountains casually show
Vancouver has a fine enough view
to challenge the world in any part
where illusionist or obsessive goes
to recover from a broken heart.

Is she asleep now? Is the sun poring
over her speech-wisdom, slipping hot money
into her marvellous mouth?
But why should I care if her nightmares flourish?
Here, I am saved – as full of self as the day before –
with pebbles and stones and rocks and mountains.
I'll scoop them up in a swoop for our favourite local
sea monster, Cadborosaurus (a little off course),
who ferries hallucinations around these waters
and makes our crazed imaginings outroar
the stupid Lions of the North Shore.
Generator of myth! Denigrator of the peace!
I'll stone your horny back clear through
Active Pass to the dotted Gulf Islands
and way into Cadboro Bay where you were first sighted
and from which you should never have strayed.
Not deep-sea monster myth, nor mother's milk,
nor love built our Columbian bones,
but stones, Mr. Cadborosaurus, stones
made this country. This country makes us stones.

SITTING

The degree of nothingness
is important:
to sit emptily
in the sun
receiving fire
that is the way
to mend
an extraordinary world,
sitting perfectly
still
and only
remotely human.

A TALL TALE

The whale, improbable as lust,
carved out a cave
for the seagirl's rest;
with rest the seagirl, sweet as dust, devised
a manner for the whale
to lie between her thighs.
Like this they lay
within the shadowed cave
under the waters, under the waters wise,
and nested there, and nested there and stayed,
this coldest whale aslant the seagirl's thighs.

Two hundred years perhaps swam by them there
before the cunning waters so distilled the pair
they turned to brutal artifacts of stone
polished, O petrified prisoners of their lair.
And thus, with quiet, submerged in deathly calm,
the two disclosed a future geologic long,
lying cold, whale to thigh revealed
the secret of their comfort
to the marine weeds,
to fish, to shell, sand, sediment and wave,
to the broken, dying sun
which probed their ocean grave.
These, whale and seagirl, stone gods,
stone lust, stone grief,
interred on the sedimented sand
amongst the orange starfish,
these cold and stony mariners
invoked the moral snail
and in sepulchral voice intoned a moral tale:

"Under the waters, under the waters wise,
all loving flesh will quickly meet demise,
the cave, the shadow cave is nowhere wholly safe
and even the oddest couple can scarcely find relief:
appear then to submit to this tide and timing sea,
but secrete a skilful shell and stone and perfect be."

SUMMER

The craft of summer
with its pander spies
to catch the whispered
wishes of its flowers

will cast its habit like
a fishing net
to draw a springtime murder
from the lake,

for summer is the incidental grave
for folly of an incidental kind,
interpolates the ice between the poles
and lays the birds against its supple wind.

SUMMER'S CAT
AS THE INEFFABLE

My cat is asleep under the tree.
She is a brief lyric
of singing fur
and, as in muted song,
the paws close and open.
To find some terrible meaning
in this round space sleeping
under the apple tree
in this grass hour
would be, perhaps, to have struck
God's thunder.
But her golden eyes are shut
and I cannot compare them.

THE CATS OF ST. IVES

contain the sea
as through their seagreen eyes
the fish of generation swim
and spin their underwater dreams,
spurning the sun of noonday lies,
chancing the life of otherwise,
here in this neatest fishing village,
here in the neutral, dozing sun.

But night sees cats all caught in change
as they remark a falling star
and idle through these idle streets
with something of Egyptian poise,
with sharpening memories of Nile.

For St. Ives' cats at night become
gods who pad on polished stone,
turning this village of quaint fishers
into a palace underwater,
letting the fishes from their eyes
to swim the temple of St. Ives
where cats all lordly roam the streets
in odd marine and feline mode
like sparkled stars through greenest weed
they thus through nights and seasons go,
ancients, a-pad their to-and-fro,
but entertain the Triton prong
against the soft, incumbent dawn.

These cats will eat and sleep and die
shaping our constant mystery;
though eyes through ages phosphoresce,
they know their temple is right now.

SEAGULLS IN A BAY

Privately moored by a first impulse
in the rocks' bay
each gull a world and privately
surveys the fish and instruments
of motion down where
earth heaves, sighs
and slowly twists
this slight ripple
and suggested fever
in the bay, the rocks' bay
where the seagulls rock and lay
their down to dance unmoving
in this cove, this hour,
this winter day.

GREY DAY

Malicious on housetops, the grey gulls
peer at our glassy lives and fluff their feathers.
It's as if they despised all that we cannot give,
and I, envying that element where they live,
screech, "Get back to that clanky sea!"
But, as if I'd said nothing at all with my seagull call,
they sit in their half-white shit,
consecrate a grey day with excremental wit.

TO FRIENDS WHO HAVE ALSO CONSIDERED SUICIDE

It's still a good idea.
Its exercise is discipline:
to remember to cross the street without looking,
to remember not to jump when the cars side-swipe,
to remember not to bother to have clothes cleaned,
to remember not to eat or want to eat,
to consider the numerous methods of killing oneself,
that is surely the finest exercise of the imagination:
death by drowning, sleeping pills, slashed wrists,
kitchen fumes, bullets through the brain or through the stomach, hanging
by the neck in attic or basement,
a clean frozen death – the ways are endless.
And consider the drama! It's better than a whole season
at Stratford when you think of the emotion of your
family on hearing the news and when you imagine
how embarrassed some will be when the body is found.
One could furnish a whole chorus in a Greek play
with expletives and feel sneaky and omniscient
at the same time. But there's no shame
in this concept of suicide.
It has concerned our best philosophers
and inspired some of the most popular
of our politicians and financiers.
Some people swim lakes, others climb flagpoles,
some join monasteries, but we, my friends,
who have considered suicide take our daily walk
with death and are not lonely.
In the end it brings more honesty and care
than all the democratic parliaments of tricks.
It is the "sickness unto death"; it is death;
it is not death; it is the sand from the beaches
of a hundred civilizations, the sand in the teeth
of death and barnacles our singing tongue:
and this is "life" and we owe at least this much
contemplation to our Western fact: to Rise,
Decline, Fall, to futility and larks,
to the bright crustaceans of the oversky.

THE EFFIGY

For if they do these things in a green tree,
what shall be done in the dry? Luke 23:31

I hoisted him up to the tree
on the ropes of my anger,
by the loops of my longing
I hooked him onto a branch.
Like a self-righteous lyncher
I had stuffed him with hatreds and visions,
but he swayed thin as the skin on a skeleton
in the polluted breeze.
Effigy of a flourishing effigy,
judicial pendulum on a time-eating tree,
he was the grandfather of grandfather clocks
and he clicked and he clocked out of me.

He was the city whose buildings leered down at me.
He was the vulgar hats of its women.
He was the pale taste of a school of Sunday painters
and the politics even I could not reform.
He was my long escape from the scary face of love
after I saw it staring from the mirror.
And then he was me searching for my *Carte d'identité*.
He was borders crossed too easily.
He was the given being not quite broken, not quite whole.
He was the No beyond negation. No!

My hands fell away. My eyes leaned up
to see my many suicides
definite in the tree.
And in this he excelled me.
There was a row of salmon gladioli in the dream
yanked out of the garden at nineteen cents a bunch,
but they too turned on me
and died without asking permission.
Therefore, take them, Strawman, for your weddings,
and swing in the motion of my sexual failures,
familiar fruit on a familiar tree.
So branch be your lullaby, so sing me free.
Pendant on your own pulp and a hard core,
hang praising now, hang praising, praising
in a green tree.

EICHMANN TRIAL

Legal beauty,
frail royalty
of mind
ritualize
the paucity of means,
the ethic not undone
by legal fiction
but nearly,
the moral structure
quaking in its boots –
self-recrimination,
oaths,
fainting,
rehearsal of sorrow
contained by the gestures
of law and the error
of structural analysis.
Simultaneity, that's the
vraie politesse:
outside the court,
blaspheming pity,
horror, tears,
storm the logicians
of dispersal,
psychotic, illegal,
the embarrassing bastard
urchins of our evil.

A LONG LINE OF BABY CATERPILLARS

A long line of baby caterpillars
follow their leader from the house corner
heading dead on for the Japanese plum tree.

Take away my wisdom and my categories!

I CAN CALL NOTHING LOVE

A smile shakes alphabets over my belly

and I bend down scrabbling "Yes" from a young Adam.

I can call nothing love that does not answer –

and I remember how Van Gogh

his own ecstatic ear cut off.

FLUX

Who would call me to still centres
needs a lesson in desire.
I am fire's ephemeral
boast on Heraclitean air.

Who would label me with names
needs my unbaptizing touch;
requisite of entities
is the constant, moving ash.

Who would kiss me on the mouth
claiming me another self
needs my body on their flesh
tasting little bites of death,

death rerising in desire
naming nothing but its hope,
spiralling in calling flights
flaming into nothing's throat.

Nothing finally is final –
every love is a rain
opening the bud to fire
asking and receiving its own Easter.

IN A GARDEN OF THE PITTI PALACE

Ripe heat falls down, persimmons burn,
an old keeper locks us in,
dangerous order, familial pain,
history intensified and sane.

Here, insolent by our side, Luca Pitti
strolls, while Piero, the Gouty Medici,
feigns sleep in that garden seat
plotting to remove Pitti from his palazzo.
The walls and fountains murmur their artificers –
Michelangelo, Tacca, Michelangelo.
Nobody dies in Italy.

But we die daily in the heat,
trailed by voices in the garden.
We have no history and hear too well.

Luca! Piero! Where can we go?
What is our reference? Why did we come
with only our private recollection
to a garden on a quiet afternoon
and Florence below explained in persimmon sun?

PAOLO AND FRANCESCA

And they laid the book aside.
The lake resumed its colour,
hills and trees cracked
from Italian sleep, motioned
but lacked that utterance
of eye and tongue;
and they laid the book aside
as hills, water, trees in their arms
they took in nature and defiance,
in humanest utterance,
and did not look aside
from that perfidious book.
The Sins of the Leopard looked
and could not look aside.

PICASSO EXHIBITION

Paris, 1954

In the simplicity of age
Picasso
comes finally to
the classical moon-
shaped faces of children
or, orbed in entire rainbows,
elliptical girls;
as for the anguished land-escaped
night, a spaghetti-haired hag
has eyes to burn out the stars –

and it is all as fierce
and angelic as the child-
hood of little Paloma and Claude.
Even before we look
we have bestowed our burdens,
preconceptions, the sense
of space and time –
even so,
in innocence they tour on vertical wheels
our darkest galleries of love;
we pause, smile, move along
to the past time of pink nudes
and blue-timed dawn.

TO A POLICEMAN
GUARDING THE NATIONAL ASSEMBLY

You strike me, Guardian, up there on your high wall,
as an archaic figure from the stiff past,
or is it more the dusty figures, tight and small,
of my own childhood, my brothers', and our last
flirtation with a land of make-believe
where toy soldiers doomed our zodiac?

I see that as you lean, Guardian, on your cold gun
(as shepherd leans on staff seeking
those lost sheep wandering in error)
your thoughts are less on duty and decrees,
the Good, subversives, gangs of terror,
than on that softest doll, your wife or girl,
tin soldier's playland and your tin desires.

Or am I wrong and you, with your straight back,
are indeed a true soldier of State,
an aim-to-fire, shoot-to-kill
sort of guy, who'll look the bomb-
packing Billy in his dynamite eyes,
pull your trigger first, then make your will?

Or you're perhaps the censor of our thoughts,
symbolizing pain, a vicious figure,
or symbolizing fences where we're caught
and tortured in no man's land, in barbed wire:
on either side the land perhaps is free
but paths to those lands all uncertainty.

Simple soldier standing on your wall,
Monsieur, in you the one contained, the all,
dreamer, shepherd, killer, criminal,
and Humpty Dumpty destined for the fall.

POEMS OF DUBLIN

I.

The sharp street-cry
    and the floating swan
the breezing rain
            deft and swift
an old man spitting blood
        I could be attracted
and compelled by this,
          Dublin city's yeasty
and outmoded brood.

II.

Yeats sent me to Parnell
and Parnell
to the murdered
in the park,

so if Yeats is living thought
and Parnell stone,
the butchered patriots
not yet undone,

there's no denying an immediate
attempt upon our liberty,
and I'm a bastard rebel full of fret,
a wild fool in Dublin on a spree

taking treacherous photographs
of innocent statues
inventing violent images to laugh
and swagger and hullabaloo

all the crazy way down
O'Connell Street and Parnell Square –
a grimace and a frown
a belch in the Irish air.

III.

The purple sash and tassel of the rhetorical heart
loudly applies itself to
the soft seduction,
the Irish mind, uneasy,
moves from where it was
to where it would be,
laughing and mocking:
the large gesture,
the flung cape,
the stage draughty
but the act good.
I'd go to Dublin any day
to hear the lilt and tilt
of a broken-down playwright
in a bookstore
and, not taking anything seriously,
not even the weather,
I'd join the ranks of "The Last Romantics."

IV.

Old Yeats, your cold, bitter,
lyrical, marble lines
drive me into innocence, the better
rage – the rest I can divine

with my "divining heart." I feel
in the cold wash of the rain
your cool and consonantal seal
upon the honeyed hive of brain –

upon everything! The Old Abbey,
swans, the priests' secret;
in St. Stephen's Green I see
ducks dock with amphibian unregret

at the pond's edge,
their heads turned back
into immediate, sensate, sinking necks
of purple and green fluffed and rebellious plumage.

SMALL SATISFACTIONS

Small satisfactions here and there
explain the slightly greying hair;
age is a cage and I go there,
hands up, nudged by a fake revolver.

Small joys and quiet ecstasies
swing me on a safe trapeze;
these fool gymnastics may appease
one with such a rare disease.

Oh, I have my dreams and visions.
I send them out on holy missions;
but they return, a cruel revision,
the bloodlust crooks of indecision.

So I take for satisfaction toys
and a daily, usual kind of boy.
It needs a ruthless, witty ploy
to check my queen, her king destroy.

A PANG CANTATA

A pang cantata
scrin of Villa-Lobos
a tinkle canticle
a rose is a rose is roses
Logos poetica Logos
Logos poetica
crin erotica!
O roaring spice
O lion of Rousseau
all exotica!
O wild canary
like a mad Chagall
hanging upon
a basil-scented wall!

TO NELLIE

"The altogetherness of everything," she said,
turning a trifle to north and south.
"Every snail's a rabbit in a train,
every cup of tea a northern gale."
She merged a little to the west
breaking her giggles into stars,
the cosmic woof went doggy at her heels,
her children sang like little cats in heat,
but skis of snowy certitude
had her already at the Pole.
Having fled her mate in spring,
she watched him going back to bed.
The winter solstice turtled on its back
and altogether everything became everything
altogether, pleasure and pain,
east, west, wind, weather,
blood into stone, roses bloomed on water,
and she, by merely thinking, had described
the gaunt circle of surprise.

OCCASIONS OF DESIRE

Occasions of desire with their attendant envies,
the white heat of the cold swan dying,
create their gestures, obscene or most beautiful.
Oh, the clear shell of a swan's fluted wings!

And as the old swan calls clarity from dark waters,
sailing triumphant into the forgotten,
desire in its moving is that rapacious cry,
gorgeous as the torrent Lethe, and as wise.

And if the curl of cygnets on the Avon,
so freshly broken from their perfect shells,
take from a dying bird not moral or enticement,
but float with their own white mother, that is just.
Oh, imperious innocence to envy
only the water bearing such beauty!

A PARDON TO MY BONES

With the prescribed number of bones
I have walked to this year,
but have despised dear bones' intent
to grow, to motivate, to be bent.
Some cracked yet show now lovely through the tent
of flesh. Although ignored, misused, can now relent
in this casual thirty-third year
because they walked me here.

Because they walked me here,
there has been gross expense
of life's uneconomic science,
of love's long argument with common sense,
a relay race from past to present tense.
The Horn of Plenty muted coming near.
And so my bones have walked me here,

Because they walked me here,
sleepwalking sightseer,
urban dirt, personal graffiti,
the indecent exposure of my city,
plucked from definite sex a baleful ditty,
moved to a pagan shout, did not come clear
because dumb bones have walked me here.

For they have walked me here.
Or we have danced or pitched in pain.
That all these bones are jointed by their hooks
I am dumbfounded as by a great book
whose leaves lie open, for illustration took
the cheating history we revere.
Bones of the appointed animal twitch the ear,
and I must be appalled, merciful, must care
that my human bones have walked me here.

POETICS AGAINST THE ANGEL OF DEATH

I am sorry to speak of death again
(some say I'll have a long life)
but last night Wordsworth's "Prelude"
suddenly made sense – I mean the measure,
the elevated tone, the attitude
of private Man speaking to public men.
Last night I thought I would not wake again
but now with this June morning I run ragged to elude
the Great Iambic Pentameter
who is the Hound of Heaven in our stress
because I want to die
writing Haiku
or, better,
long lines, clean and syllabic as knotted bamboo. Yes!

Naked Poems

star fish

fish star

Suite 1

MOVING

to establish distance
between our houses.

It seems
I welcome you in.

Your mouth blesses me
all over.

There is room.

AND
here
and here and
here
and over   and
over   your mouth

TONIGHT
quietness.   In me
and the room.

I am enclosed
by a thought

and some walls.

THE BRUISE

Again you have left
your mark.

Or we
have.

Skin shuddered
secretly

FLIES

tonight
in this room
two flies
on the ceiling
are making
love
quietly.   Or

so it seems
down here

YOUR BLOUSE

I people
this room
with things, a
chair,   a lamp,   a
fly two books by
Marianne Moore.

I have thrown my
blouse on the floor.

Was it only
last night?

YOU
took

with so much
gentleness

my dark

Suite II

While you were away

I held you like this
in my mind.

It is a good mind
that can embody
perfection with exactitude.

The sun comes through
plum curtains.

I said
the sun is gold

in your eyes.

It isn't the sun
you said.

On the floor your blouse.
The plum light
falls more golden

going down.

Tonight
quietness
in the room.

We knew

Then you must go.
I sat cross-legged
on the bed.
There is no room
for self-pity
I said

I lied

In the gold darkening
light

you dressed.

I hid my face
in my hair.

The room that held you

is still here

You brought me clarity.

Gift after gift
I wear.

Poems   naked

in the sunlight

on the floor.

Non Linear

An instant of white roses.
          Inbreathing.
A black butterfly's
          twitch and determined
collapse on a yellow round.

near the white Tanabe
narcissus
near Layton's *Love*
daffodils
outside   falling on
the pavement
the plum blossoms
of Cypress Street

the yellow chrysanthemums

    (I hide my head when I sleep)

a stillness
in jade

    (Your hand reaches out)

the chrysanthemums

are

    (Job's moaning, is it, the dark?)

a whirlwind!

Eros!   *Agapé*   *Agapé*

Her sickness does not ebb
anyhow, it's not a sea
it's a lake largely
        moon-ridden.

I can see her perfectly clearly
through this dusk her face
the colour of moonlight.

Maybe my body, maybe I?
But when has my love
                ever been

offered exactly
and why should she be an
                exception?

walking in dark

waking in dark the presence of all

the absences we have known.   Oceans.

so we are distinguished to ourselves

don't want that distinction.

I am afraid. I said that. I said that

for you.

My white skin
is not the moonlight.
If it is
tell me, who reads
by that light?

a curve / broken
of green
moss weed
kelp shells pebbles
lost orange rind
orange crab   pale
delicates at peace
on this sand
tracery of last night's
tide

I am listening for
the turn of the tide
I imagine it will sound
an appalled sigh
the sigh of Sisyphus
who was not happy

Hieratic sounds emerge
from the Priestess of
Motion
a new alphabet
gasps for air.

We disappear in the musk of her coming.

I hear the waves
hounding the window:
lord, they are the root waves
of the poem's metre
the waves of the
root poem's sex.
The waves of Event
(the major planets, the minor
planets, the Act)
break down at my window:
I also hear those waves.

the dead dog now
the one I saw last night
carried on a man's shoulders
down to the beach
he held it by its
dead crossed legs

I have given up
complaining

but nobody
notices

"That ye resist not
evil" falling
limp into the arms
of the oppressor
he is not undone
by the burden
of your righteousness
he has touched you

Suite of Lies

I know the way
of the pear tree
and apple tree the way
the light shines
through pear petal
apple, a light
falling into our
consanguinity

brother and sister
conjunctive and
peaceable

I use the word groves
light falling
found in the orchard
finding what fell by a
breath

brother and sister
those children

the way of what fell
the lies
like the petals
falling   drop
delicately

Some final questions

What are you sad about?

that all my desire goes
out to the impossibly
beautiful

Why are you standing there staring?

I am watching a shadow
shadowing a shadow

Now you are sitting doubled up in pain.
What's that for?

doubled up I feel
small like these poems
the area of attack
is diminished

What do you really want?

want the apple on the bough in
the hand in the mouth seed
planted in the brain want
to think "apple"

I don't get it. Are you talking about
process and individuation. Or absolutes
whole numbers that sort of thing?

Yeah

But why don't you do something?

I am trying to write a poem

Why?

Listen. If I have known beauty
let's say I came to it
asking

Oh?

Wilson's Bowl

for John and Sally Hulcoop

"I am both too big and too weak for writing. I am *alongside* it, for writing is always dense, violent, indifferent to the infantile ego which solicits it." I was so grateful to Roland Barthes when I discovered that passage in *A Lover's Discourse* because it so perfectly describes my relationship to writing, and I don't think I could ever myself have explained the bloodline with such precision. My poems are born out of great struggles of silence. This book has been long in coming. Wayward, natural, and unnatural silences, my desire for privacy, my critical hesitations, my critical wounds, my dissatisfactions with myself and the work have all contributed to a strange gestation. And in the meantime a projected work begun in 1967 became a small literary legend. *The Kropotkin Poems* were never completed. Too grand and too designed (the "body politic" and "love's body" as interchangeable polymorphous analogues in an ideal world), they were perhaps too big and too weak for me. The infantile ego could not solicit that beautiful anarchist dream poem. Violence, density, indifference did not presume to speak. Neither the Muse of History nor the Muse of Poetry nor the "towering dead" could move me through that work. But there are remnants of its beginning in a study of power contained in this collection among the *Portraits* and the *Crimes* and the *Poems of Failure*.

Having dealt with one apologia, I must now deal with another, which is really more of an embarrassment to myself than anything else. And that is the dominance of male figures in *Portraits*. These poems were not written as a group, nor at one time, but spread over many years, like the silence. Some have suggested that these figures could be masks, personae, my animus, my male muse in many guises. I wonder and I think. I think that those interpretations are significant – I might even agree with them. They signify the domination of a male power culture in my educational and emotional formation so overpowering that I have, up to now, been denied access to inspiration from the female figures of my intellectual life, my heart, my imagination. The "Letters to Margaret Atwood" are an exception; I was *asked* to write on the subject of women that time. The others – the unwritten poems – are the real "poems of failure."

P.W., Salt Spring Island, B.C., June 16, 1980

Preface

POEMS OF FAILURE

I.

A picture of sweet old Prince
Kropotkin on the wall

will the little lady fall from
her chair?

"Our Meeting" out of Goodman
out of *The Empire City*

knowledge? that we are
inconsolable

and now take off from there
to leave the Flying Dutchman
coming home

let the Prince hang
the little lady float

is there a shadow following the
hand that writes
always? or for the left-handed
only?

I cannot write with my right.

I grasp what I can. The rest
is a great shadow.

Nevertheless, when the boat
moves through the islands
pushes clumsily into the dock
another chapter is written
shadow moves up the gang
plank with us is Chapter
7, 11, 13?

To be reconciled with the past
is redemption but unreal as hell
if you can't recall the beginning
and of time, who can get back there?

redemptive anthropologists, archae-
ologists, bones, stones, rings of
trees …

The old Prince hangs on the
wall, rain-stained edges
of the portrait

and there – up goes the little lady
and – no shadow falls

"Loyal to the silence of our impasse …
we look at each other … we do not go …
in the faith that we are inconsolable …
we are resting in this hell."

II.

Incredible fire, irresistible grace
k, k, k, kaw, kaw.
The burning on the hillside, ineffable
smoke, "what does not change is
the will to change"
k, k, k, kaw
the drummers' drums echoing across
the bay, they won't go away
drums or echoes.
Insurrectionary wilderness of the I
am, I will be, forcing the vision
to something other, something out
side the sleep of dreams riddled
with remembrances.
k, k, k, the Prince in his dungeon
exploring his way
why is he so saintly, the reaches
of his mind so vast and intimate?
("The main structural lines of Asia are not
north and south, or west and east; they are
from the *southwest to the northeast* ...")
Kropotkin, old Prince Peter
with your forty barges on the Amur
with your hammer in Finland
dressed up in your merchant's costume
dressed up as a *page de chambre*
dressed up as an eight-year old Persian
Prince with real jewels in your belt for
Madame Nazimova "who was a very beautiful
woman." Peter, sweet Prince for Nicholas
for Alexander ("and have signed myself ever
since P. Kropotkin.")
And your Alexander, your brother, suicided
in Siberia.
Peasants in the field
the Jura watchmakers scooping out lids

you writing, speaking, hoeing your garden
greeting your friends, your mind sent out
to the people, a movement turning me to you
40 years after Sacco and Vanzetti
50th anniversary of the Russian Revolution
your gentle words wounding me on this island,
"even now, as I was looking on the lakes and
the hillocks of Finland, new and beautiful gener-
alizations arose before my eyes ... But what
right had I to these highest joys?"

III.

Guarding me is not enough. Nor my own guardianship.
Take it all away, I can walk.
What is locked in nevertheless pounds
at the gates (he dropped his dressing gown,
one-two and ran through the gates, the
violinist in the little grey house speeding
him with a mazurka). Do we need a guide?
Garrulous voices offend, deny, kick, condemn
what the other offers. Head bows in pain to the
blows. The ears turn off. I will not listen.
I shall not speak. Tap, tap. Tap, tap, tap.
Prisoners in the St. Peter and St. Paul fortress
sending their telex messages.
Raving below the Prince, a peasant
goes mad in his cell. The Prince is listening.
As above, so below.
I slow my lines.
I walk up and down the room which looks out
on islands and strait and do not protest
"what right have I to these highest joys?"
But my "good masterpiece of work" does not come
"between all the harmonies of the mother nature,
under the radiant rays of sun when everything grows
so vividly in the human mind and in the heart,
love, life and all the vegetation beautifully ..."
                    Sacco, Dedham Jail
            November 26th, 1926
writing to his dear friend Mrs. Jack.

IV.

Shall I tell you what I do to pass the time
here on the island at night?
There is red velvet and purple velvet.
I cut out diamonds from a pattern piece
by piece. I sew two pieces, one purple
one red, together, attach another making designs
as I go. Mapping it into some kind of crazy
poncho. I am absorbed in the fitting together
of pieces. Troika the white cat watches.
Red velvet on purple purple on red colours
of the mystic and revolutionary. *The Politics
of Experience, Love's Body, Psycho-
pathology and Politics,* Trotsky's *Journal,* Pushkin,
*The Possessed, Social Contract, Journey into Russia,
Memoirs of a Revolutionist, The Romantic Exiles,
Anarchism.* "Eleanor Rigby."

Far out in the strait low star lights of the
ferry boats follow a radar map.

The cat jumps on my lap. She stares.

V.

Away from everything, alone with a road
map of Salt Spring Island
I drive spitting dust with a map
of the U.S.S.R. in my head. Too big
for my head. Too big to remember how many
independent republics, airlines routes, rivers,
mountain ranges, lakes, and all named places.
I speed on covering the highspots up to the
north end back to my southeast Beaver Point.
Back home in front of the fireplace I wonder
Russia, Suicide or France? I am aware.
Darkness pulls over the islands.
Russia, Suicide or France. Islands, places
on a map. Nowhere.

VI.

Dream: September 7th, 1967. Salt Spring Island.
How do you ever find anything here, I asked Arthur Erickson,
having walked through his long house. The rooms had
numbers on the doors. I was not impressed with the
architecture but I was by the seascape, and said so.
Perfectly easy, he replied, and reached out to show me
a ring which was more like a bracelet, it was so big.
A rectangle of ancient yellow metal inlaid with smaller
rectangles. There were little antique holes all part
of the pattern. I turned it over to find inscribed:
Russia, 1965.

Dream: September 11th, 1967. Salt Spring Island.
I find my cat outside the house. Dead. She has been killed
by a rat by a bite on the throat. She lies there, white
and dead. The black rat leans against her. I wake up
and call Troika Troika, but she's not on the bed. The
light turn on the light. She is sniffing happily in
the firewood. Troika!

"Else a great prince in prison lies."

Today (September 13th, 1967) I smoked pot in the afternoon,
something had to be done, no effect. I went out in
the boat and rowed a little. The drops of water, silver,
falling from the left oar. I went offcourse watching.
Then gathered bark and came back. The sun is shining.
The arbutus groves and pines send messages, tap, tap,
tap, as the bark and needles fall.

VII.

The memoirs of a revolutionist before me, things fall
together now. Pine needles, arbutus bark, the tide
comes in, path to the beach lights with sun-fall.
Highest joys? The simple profundity of a dead man works
at my style. I am impoverished. He the White Christ.
Not a case of identification. Easier to see myself
in the white cat asleep on the bed. Exile. I live
alone. I have a phone. I shall go to Russia. One
more day run round and the "good masterpiece of work"
does not come. I scribble. I approach some distant dream.
I wait for moonlight reflecting on the night sea. I can
wait. We shall see.

from *The Kropotkin Poems*, 1967

Portraits

SOCRATES

Scientia
immaculata
I ignoramus
fiddling with
the lives of
the great
think Socrates
occasionally
a fool taking
logic for truth
likewise numerology
is not statistics
but helpful magic
in all such systems
to open the
eye of the soul
as Socrates said
being careful not
to blind it
however looking
on essences.
Now I suspect
claritas
hid from shadows
it alone cast
as it fell
upon objects
laying up
luminescence
through layers
of the ethereal
mindstuff
and for alternatives

hard-edged
heavens and
hells
slumbering on both
sides of the golden
mean. On the last
day gathered together
in his prison cell
they discussed these
matters they were
clever and even
gentle with one
another exemplary
students for the
old master
about to go who
stroking Phaedo's
locks laid a bet
(or an oath?)
concerning the length
of hair.
Whoever died like that
with such good manners?
Such elegance of
speech and
intricacy of thought?
The absolute
business
of the state
settled
good citizen Socrates
law-abiding to the
bitter end liberating
his soul through
sweet philosophy

his major music
chorded harmoniously
pluck   pluck
tuned and ready to
fly with its eye
wide open for
a new spectrum
securing melodious
ultraviolet and
infrared
through the tip
of each wing.
The cup of hemlock
doesn't seem to cause
pain to the old man
under the blanket
in his cell surrounded
by friends. He remembers
a last obligation
(legs and torso numb)
pokes out his head
to tell Crito: "I owe
a cock to Asclepius:
will you remember
to pay the debt?"
Even his last words
a question.
What a dumb play
for one who knew
all the answers
his questions
were answers.
"For is not philosophy
the study of death?"

Consider the dead
for whom we make elegies
how they differently
instruct us.
I have been studying
K. on his deathbed
a pine frond arranged
into the photographer's
lustrous design
and lace and a white
pillow for bedding death
for a still life
incidental to the grand
pianos hammering out
in Moscow and Petrograd
love domiciled in lace
pine & pillow in Dmitrov
in Dmitrov a son of man
domesticated, a wild idea
whose face is noble
and kindly, a prince
of a man waxing into
a death's head
a great dome, home
his *Ethics* unfinished ...
the reaches of his mind
so vast and intimate ...
O Socrate! ("la langue
paralysée et suis
incapable ...")
his white beard
where the morning stars
sang ...

FOR FYODOR

I am a beetle in the cabbage soup they serve up for geniuses
in the House of the Dead.

I am a black beetle and loll seductively at the bottom of the
warm slop.

Someday, Fyodor, by mistake you'll swallow me down and I'll become
a part of your valuable gutworks.

In the next incarnation I hope to imitate that idiot and saint,
Prince Myshkin, drop off my wings for his moronic glory.

Or, if I miss out on the Prince, Sonya or Dunya might do.

I'm not joking. I am not the result of bad sanitation in the
kitchen, as you think.

Up here in Omsk in Siberia beetles are not accidents but destinies.

I'm drowning fast, but even in this condition I realize your bad-
tempered haughtiness is part of your strategy.

You are about to turn this freezing hell into an ecstatic emblem.
A ferocious shrine.

Ah, what delicious revenge. But take care! A fit is coming!
Now, now I'll leap into your foaming mouth and jump your tongue.
Now I stamp on this not quite famous tongue

shouting: Remember, Fyodor, you may hate men but it's here in
Omsk you came to love mankind.

But you don't hear, do you: there you are writhing in epileptic
visions.

Hold your tongue! You can't speak yet. You are mine, Dostoevsky.

I aim to slip down your gullet and improve myself.
I can almost hear what you'll say:

> Crime and Punishment
> Suffering and Grace

and of the dying

> pass by and forgive
> us our happiness

And among the divine paranoids old Ezra
paces his cage unattached to the mode of doubt
replete with salvation he is 60 years old
under the Pisan sunfire. He sees straight
through the bars into the court of Confucius
then slumps in a corner wondering what went
wrong. His old man's hair is matted with rain
and wardust. His brain is in fever.
Nevertheless he hikes from pole to pole
to plot once more the stars of his fixed
obsession. It seems so clear. If only
they'd listened. They shine light all night
on the perplexity of his predicament.
He stares back, can't sleep, understands
nothing. Jew-hater. Poet. Intellectual.
A curious animal, atypical, it reads and
writes, shaking and sweating, being so shut in,
the canto arising:
 "And if the corn can be beaten
  Demeter has lain in my furrow"
the mode of doubt imprisoned for ever and ever
in the style of its own luxury.

RILKE

Rilke, I speak your name I throw it away
with your angels, your angels, your statues
and virgins, and a horse in a field held
at the hoof by wood. I cannot take so much
tenderness, tenderness, snow falling like lace
over your eyes year after year as the poems
receded, roses, the roses, sinking in snow
in the distant mountains.

Go away with your women to Russia or take them
to France, and take them or don't the poet is
in you, the spirit, they love that.
(I met one in Paris, her death leaning outward,
death in all forms. The letters you'd sent her,
she said, stolen from a taxi.)

Rilke.
Clowns and angels held your compassion.
You could sit in a room saying nothing,
nothing. Your admirers thought you were there,
a presence, a wisdom. But you had to leave
everyone once, once at least. That was your
hardness.

This page is a shadowed hall in Duino Castle.
Echoes. The echoes.
I don't know why I'm here.

FATHER

The light is mauve
my eye's iris blooms
into the nightmare of
riderless horse, the sleep honey
sings through the lilac
and I smell ash.
I touch the skin of the
horse, his pelt, thinking
of Father's military ride
Father's pomaded hair brushed
back, brown, and his long beautiful
hands holding the reins
just so, horse dancing.
And at the end, Father
smiling his great Rosicrucian smile
sniffing the light
flicked whip of lilac
his eyes seeing beyond me
the Rosy Cross.

VASARELY

for Ann Richardson

Vasarely arrives through the mail
disguised as a postcard from Aix-en-
Provence, Detroit, or Tallahassee, Fla.
He is hiding his secret vice in a cube
of mauve.

I am wrong. Vasarely is a red telephone box.
No. Vasarely is in a telephone box (blue).
He is dialing Tridim-C 1968 – *Allo! Allo!*
He connects with Tallahassee and Saturday's
death in the afternoon opera.
"Pourquoi es-tu si triste ma chère?"
He is death in the afternoon.

Vasarely is no longer in his green telephone box.
He is in Sri Lanka standing on his head.
He sticks out his tongue and wriggles
his fingers in his ears.
He hates Wagner. He disappears.

He is, perhaps, an opening on
the invisible – *Allo … Allo …*

He dials again (in his index finger
the fingerprints of Mars):
"Tu es dégoutante, ma soeur!
You are the one I blame." He hangs
up smiling.
I myself have brown eyes

I shift my gaze from the abode of adoration.

Ach! He is a grey gnome in a playpen
dribbling integers crying
for the holy spectrum.
I would freeze him into a tray of ice cubes
but he'd only look out at me
with his aqua eyes.

He's out and scuttling around the corner
passing among the archangels and their
sibling rivals – *Allo ... allo ...*
dicing for multiples of eleven.

(*Pourquoi es-tu si triste?*)

He is withdrawn again into the
Everlasting, studying his *Book of
Changes*, his horrendous hexagrams.
He is laughing and laughing.

And only yesterday I thought I saw
him painting himself into a corner
(ochre). He caught me looking.
He hopped up the ladder
and then he came down.
He fanned a pack of red.
It laid me low. It said:

"*Pourquoi es-tu si triste, chérie?
C'est toujours moi.
C'est moi. C'est Vasarely!*"

Dear Peggy: What follows is a sort of hollow-eyed celebration. I couldn't make it to champagne, balloons, and funny hats. You will understand why. Am I responding to your books or you? If it's your books, then I can name them: *Survival, Surfacing, Power Politics.* If it's you, then it's a possibly odd, possibly even perception of you. The energy to do anything at all, and I have to admit it isn't much, came mainly from *Survival*. It made me feel good. The whole sickness laid bare, making sense, allowing no further excuses. So Ice Virgin, Stone Angel, Paralyzed Artist, and repentant Hecate (I deceive you only a little) got off her couch and wrote some "Letters to Margaret Atwood from Phyllis Webb."

*   *   *

Peggy, they say yours is an "astonishing cruel talent" and that you have very little love for anything. They're wrong. It's just that you say what they don't want to hear and the assured form of it, the cold uncomfort, hurts them. You don't know where to find deluding smiles or Barbie Doll tears or the Baby *Ex Machina*. That's not what you're looking for anyhow. When you said, "Where is here?" they ripped open your heart to watch the emergence of one more bloody animal victim, hoping it would give them an accusing but tender look before it died in the tradition. When they ripped you screamed a lovely diatonic scream, briefly, and then explained that the heart is a valve for pumping blood and that was your heart and your blood and they could get the hell out while you sewed it back in place. "What a woman, what a cool surgeon," they murmured, almost in awe. Vague pictures of Dr. Norman Bethune floated before them as he worked and worked and worked and became a national hero to the Chinese Communists because he was a good doctor and knew where he was needed.

*   *   *

I refuse to publish because I refuse to write. What I've written I hoard, hoping the poems will eventually turn into satisfactory failures. I've been preparing the model *in vitro* for years. There's some chance of success. They may yet roll over like dead dogs, howling, "We never wanted to be poems anyhow," which I think is a line by Leonard Cohen. So I'll leave a legacy of buried verbs, a tight-mouthed treasure. Someday when you require more evidence you can dig them up, my bones, cross-hatched with grim messages. I even give permission for them to be displayed under glass in the National Museum in Ottawa, otherwise known as the Great Canadian Coffin.

*   *   *

Dear Peggy: I have news for you. The Stone Angels are crumbling in the cemetery. The Ice Virgins melted last spring and became a deep green pool full of rainbow trout which they are trying very hard to love. The Earth Mothers restrain themselves during full moon. They are now members of Zero Population Growth. They grew tired of their mythic proportions. Hecate still frowns and pulls down her mouth but she has shortened her skirts to reveal a fantastic pair of legs which she's been hiding – righteously and reluctantly – for years. Diana and Venus are OK – on the pill and sleeping around. They look delicious. "It's good," they say and are willing to prove it. "Give us a paralyzed artist," they chime it out like the heavenly twins: "Give us a paralyzed artist or two." Peggy, I tell you they're plotting to change the course of Canadian Literature and you're going to have to write another book.

*   *   *

Whatever happened to The News of the World? It became autobiography. Someday I will explode and you will explode in another damned Apocalypse. Or I will slowly suffocate and become ugly And you will slowly suffocate and say, "I told you so."

*   *   *

Peggy: When I see pictures of you in your old fur coat I think maybe you've jumped into an animal skin so you can hide where you always wanted to be. But then I remember you said an animal cannot be separated from its skin painlessly. If you can tolerate both ideas at once, then, like me, you eat meat and, as knife and fork are raised in benediction, amazed eyes at the slaughterhouse follow you, and you taste a quick stun on a shining place.

*   *   *

After survival, what? The sedition in my own hand, will it be written down legibly, will I sign it and hand it over for someone else to fulfill? Or will I open like a Venus flytrap to catch fat spies from the enemy lines and feed myself forever on them on them on them? They really aren't worth my exotic trouble but I can't eat money and I want for once to be useful.

*   *   *

Peggy: Sometimes I hear you screaming between the paragraphs and poems. That doesn't really bother me. Screams should be heard and not seen. And anyhow the poems and paragraphs eventually proceed before the amorous invisible, governed by need and the form of its persuasions.

Crimes

SOLITARY CONFINEMENT

It is a delusion.
The cell is not quiet.
A tree falls in the forest
with no one to hear.
The forest is falling.
It hears itself.
The rain ineluctable
speechless and necessary.
The cell is a green tower
maggoty   damp   a sickness
being offered.
It is just a cell like any
other cell   barred
hard   very   principled
and guarded.
Let my tongue hang out
to remember the thirst for life.
Let my tongue hang out
to deliver itself
of the bitter curd.
And spit
give me water for spit.
Then give me
a face.

STILL THERE ARE WARS AND CRIMES OF WAR

war crimes war crimes war cries cries war
war cries war cries cries cry crimes cry
crimes cry cry cries cries cry war cries
war crimes crimes crimes crime cries war
cries war war war war warm cries warm cries
cries cries cries cries still there are war
war war war still still warm cries still warm
warm warm cries CRIES WAR CRIES there are there
are still still still still still

TREBLINKA GAS CHAMBER

Klostermayer ordered another count of the children.
Then their stars were snipped off and thrown into
the center of the courtyard. It looked like a field of
buttercups. – JOSEPH HYAMS, *A Field of Buttercups*

fallingstars
          "a field of
                    buttercups"

               yellow stars
                         of David
                                   falling

the prisoners
               the children
                         falling

          in heaps
                    on one another
                              they go down

Thanatos
          showers
                    his dirty breath
                              they must breathe
                                        him in

               they see stars
                         behind their
                                   eyes

David's
     "a field of
               buttercups"

          a metaphor
                    where all that's
                              left lies down

FROM *THE KROPOTKIN POEMS*

Syllables disintegrate ingrate alphabets
               lines decline into futures and limbos
                       intentions and visions fall

and fall like bad ladders.

I shaft my needle again and again
               into hell's veins and heaven's
                       listening for messages pulsing

on whose bloody hopes?

Whose love, tell me, O love's divine airs
                       elaborates the oratorio?

His dream. His exile. His imprisonments. Shadows

of his brother fixed in handiwork, letters, lexicons,

                       lessons, bereavements.

                       Alexander.

And him growing old. Peter. Who loved him before his marriage
at age thirty-six? Who did he lust for or sleep with
and who shifted his decorous sweetness into plain-song
                       pain-song, body to body?

                       Peter.

The state of affairs so bad, the sufferings
                          power in things awry
                                              crooked
and perilous orders, forcing his language.

He cut his own vein
                stateless in grace
                                  O love words flow

on love whose airs are his own oratorio.

                          In Adam's garden

he plants all his blood.

■

Three?
       Mile?
            Island?

A QUESTION OF QUESTIONS

I.

question
query
hook
    of the soul
    a question of
questions
        why / how
          oh God
        has it come to this

hook
sickle
scythe
    to cut us down this
mark?
    who – how many years
    to shape the mind to make
    its turn toward this?
    the where / when of the type
    the proper fall of lead
    in the printer's font?
    and who are you in this
school
room
torture chamber
    whose are you?
    and what of your
    trials and errors?
the judge
    in his echo chamber
    cannot know
    and nor can you
    you cannot answer

II.

Succulent lobe of the ear
droplet of flesh
depending from the not
quite crescent you are
allowed to hear with.
Does it know what I say?
Can it imagine my sentence?
I bring my head near.
I whisper.
I flicker my tongue in tricks.
I taste the stare of its mischief.
I riddle my enterprise.
I shut my mouth and open my eyes.
Suddenly I do not love
that ornament, that place.
Turn your head.
I want to see your face.

III.

The hello of your mouth is what I want
the smile of your crooked pearlies.
Whatever *is* rustles existence out of some
mouth, stuffs essence into some other.
          Fancy talk
              in the continuum
                  of my wanting
              a word / the word / the
          occult withdrawn-ness of it
              I endure that
                      or suffer busy-
            bodies' oneway chatter
                fools of time ungladly.
Hello / hello is as equal as we'll come
                  my love
              my question
          my answer
              smiles on one side,
ugly, or other of
              power and seduction.
Scene / Riviera
      villa's shutters clap and boo Monsieur
              Sun, Mistral, Peeping
    Tom who want my names
          your many occupations.
Let's shutter ourselves in sleep.
    (Where did your mouth go?
        why didn't you say hello?)

Dark, take their inquisition.
    Thinking, at best,
            is dreaming
                    chase and quarry
        hounds at bay
                    horses and riding masters
the decay of all that
        into morning
                where nothing is
        not over, never done with
                once and for all
                        All eyes!
I remember my dream of last night's raiding cops
who judged my lovemaking for a contest.
The night before you stunned a Minister
of Justice, who must have passed the word.
I can't answer for nuance and spectrum.
The case doesn't hold.
Try wearing a ring
        try going for aquamarine and losing.
Or. Topaz. Opal. Ultras. Primes.
        The pigments of Bosch
                    dismay the drift of your
                        nightmare
my waves of Dufy.
        Sleep on my love, my lovely.
I'll hum the blues. I'll monologue
        Our little lives …
                    Our voluptuous questing …

IV.

Extracted toenails.
I have nothing to say.

Burns on the breasts.
I have nothing to say.

Electric shock.
I have nothing to say.

Beatings.
I have nothing to say.

Refinements of an old skill.
Make the inner outer.

I am what I am.
All one.

Done. Take it away.

V.

for R.D.L.

The error lies in
the state of desire
in wanting the answers
wanting the red-crested
woodpecker to pose
among red berries
of the ash tree
wanting its names
its habitations
the instinct
of its ways for
my head-travelling
wanting its colours
its red, white, its black
pressed behind my eyes
a triptych
three-fold
and over
and wanting the bird
to be still and
wanting it moving
whiteflash of underwings
dazzling all questions
out of me, amazement
and outbreathing
become a form
of my knowing.

I move and it moves
into a cedar tree.
I walk and I walk.
My deceiving angel's
in-shadow joins me
paces my steps and threatens
to take my head
between its hands.

I keep walking.
Trying to think.
Here on the island
there is time
on the Isabella
Point Road.
We pass a dead
deer on the beach.
Bloated. It stinks.
The angel insists, "Keep
walking. It has all the time
in the world. Is sufficient.
Is alone. Keep walking,"
it says and flies off
with my head.

What's left of me
remembers a funny song
also a headless
man on rockface
painted in red
by Indian finger spirits.

The red-crested woodpecker swoops down
and sits on my trunk. Posing.
Dryocopus pileatus. "Spectacular, black,
crow-sized woodpecker with a red *crest*,
great size, sweeping wingbeats, flashing
white underwing." Pileated woodpecker.
Posing. Many questions.
"The diggings, large *oval* or *oblong* holes,
indicate its presence."

Zen Master.

I am wearing absent-minded red
slippers and a red vest –
spots of blood
to match the broken English
of Count Dracula being interviewed
on the radio in the morning sun.
I touch the holes in my throat
where the poppies bud – spots of blood
spots of womantime. "14,000 rats,"
Dracula is saying, and the interviewer
echoes, "14,000 rats! So beautiful,"
he sighs, "The Carpathian Mountains –
the photography, so seductive!" The Count
also loves the film; he has already seen it
several times. He tells in his dreamy voice
how he didn't need direction, didn't want
makeup, how he could have done it with his own
teeth. He glided in and out of this role
believing in reincarnation, in metamorphosis.
Yet 14,000 rats and the beleaguered
citizens of the Dutch town where those scenes
were shot (without him) are of no interest.
"And Hollywood?" the interviewer asks, himself
an actor, 'Hollywood next?' Who knows?
Who knows?

The blood pounds at my temples.
The women of the world parade before me
in red slippers and red vests, back and
forth, back and forth, fists clenched.
My heart emerges from my breast for
14,000 rats and the citizens of Delft,
for the women of the world in their menses.

Yet I too imitate a crime of passion:
Look at these hands. Look at the hectic
red painting my cheekbones as I metamorphose
in and out of the Buddha's eye, the *animus
mundi.*

In the morning sun Count Dracula leans
against my throat with his own teeth.
Breathing poppies. Thinking.

FREE TRANSLATIONS

I.

Raven did not come on Thursday.
He sent nothing.
Not a word. Not a sign.
Nothing on Thursday. Nothing on Friday. Nothing
on Saturday. Nothing on Sunday.
Then he sent eagles.

II.

Raven has blue eyes, like the waters of the
Queen Charlotte Islands on a good day.
He also carries a black magic umbrella.
This makes me want to sing. Caw caw.
Or cry.

III.

Raven is just a baby
floating in his cradle on the sea.
He bides his time sucking his wing
and dreaming of stone tits.
He is going to create something
great when he grows up:
the world first, ha ha.
And then his mother.

IV.

Raven has all the girls he needs.
He's got machismo and charisma.
He sings Cole Porter songs in the shower
and thinks he's James Cagney.
When he's dry he plays the piano
choosing a Chopin nocturne, so touching.

V.

Raven's got everything going for him.
He's riding high.
He says he's going to steal the sun.
Why not the sun?

Then we can all shine.

Artifacts

WILSON'S BOWL

in memory of Lilo, who walked into the sea,
January 1977, Salt Spring Island

"You may read my signs
but I cross my path
and show you nothing
on your way."

FOUND POEM

Duende
Dark song
"does not appear
if it sees no possibility
of death."

Duende
"Likes a straight fight
with the creator
on the edge of the well."

Duende
"Where is the *Duende*?
An air smelling of a child's
saliva, of pounded grass
announcing the constant
baptism of newly created
things."

Duende
Dark sounds
"behind which we discover
volcanoes, ants, soft
winds, the Milky Way."

"It burns the blood
like powdered glass."
Duende!

Thus Lorca, his *Duende*.
Over the world
Duende.

In this place
Tremendum.

THE BOWL

This is not a bowl you drink from not a loving
cup.
This is meditation's place
cold rapture's.
Moon floats here
belly, mouth, open-one-eye
any orifice
comes to nothing
dark as any mask
or light, more light / is
holy *cirque.*
Serene, it says silence
in small fish
cups a sun
holds its shape
upon the sea
howls, "Spirit entered
black as any raven."
Smiles –
and cracks your smile.
Is clean.

SHE SINGS

"Over the holy water the dedication.
Over the holy water the syllables.
Over the holy water equations.
Over the holy water the golden disc
settles (mercy and loving-beholding).
Noble the mathematics, the calculations.
Noble the old rock asleep and beyond our tears."

IN THIS PLACE

The spirits are not benign
up on Mt. Erskine chittering
at fog-flyers
up on Mt. Maxwell with cougar
who spies out the lambs of Musgrave.
Up on Mt. Bruce mean spirits
scrabble radio waves
for living and dead.
They doze on Mt. Tuam.
They never sleep.
At full moon
they come down on the rocks
of the sea's shore
deliver such messages:
are not gone.
We quake. We draw curtains
against the word's blaze.

She goes out on the water
hearing.
Is taken or given
by tides.
I go as far as I can
collaborating in the fame.

Her scheme of last minutes
her strategies
are little songs
for great earth
(to which I listen carefully
in this place).

■

"I took the path,
I crossed the signs.

I crossed the path.
I took the signs."

Dark sounds.
Dark sounds.

What was the path she took?
As winding as her gut
with the pain in it?
Along the beach?
To the caves in the hill?
Path of her mind turning
on symbols. Civility and
the Wild Woman's scream.
And horror. Horror.
Path to the beach
at full moon at last
joy of that mean water,
the manic ride out in the bay.

■

"O air, I beat my wings
against you
against great songs
of little earth
O air!"

TWIN MASKS

I ask if a woman could have made them
the two stone masks
that can nest together
one with its eyes open
one with its eyes closed.
Did Wilson ever think of that
before he shot himself so tidily
in his office?
I think of it and feel the weight
of the rock reject me.
For the dance! For the dance!
O stone, I hold whatever hands
that held you. O stone, we hold
this hour together under the artful
light of the gallery.
I stand here reading the lies
of paradox, reading the eyes
which have not worn you since
they flashed in the fires of
the longhouse and went out –
dancing!

Black bird pecks at her ear
pushes through to a nest in her brain.
She hears heavy feathers twice:
once as riffs on a drum;
once as a black bird's sigh.

IMPERFECT SESTINA

I.

So what if Lowry got spooked by seabirds and volcanoes crossing,
his alterego stood beside him in the double mirror,
showed him Eden and flapped off darkest Raven,
who, cawing, took her mask and showed his twin.
Who can survive that mad illumination
shining in eyes, pouring over the stone.

II.

We who have dreamt our demons into stone,
caught at our groins, screamed and fell at the crossing,
find mercy and loving-beholding illumination.
Hide the mirrors. Break them. There are more mirrors.
See how the crucial stork rides off with its twin.
Over the world the Paraclete, the holy Raven.

III.

Mind you, there may be more to a bird than its name Raven.
I have often wondered about a rhyme with stone.
There is a nest and there is nesting and something about the
                              birthday of a twin.
I have seen both open and closed eyes at the double crossing,
and even as I lay there dying I saw the mirror.
Shall you or I smash out that multiple illumination?

IV.

Oh yes, Death came, and, oh yes, there was illumination.
Death sang a song, one grand delusion of Raven
got up in feathers and a mask of stone.
Now give me back that mirror, give me the mirror,
and I will show the path and why it is a crossing.
And you and I shall lie there buying illumination.

V.

Did I say buying illumination? Illumination,
twin beat of flinty wings, one-eyed illumination?
Can I really say I found even two cents at the crossing?
There I was stabbed and pecked by spirit Raven.
There in that marriage I turned into stone,
and did not understand he carved me at his mirror.

VI.

Six times six I multiplied the vision by the mirror.
Now any mask can show me all those twins.
Loving-beholding and mercy pecked upon a stone
until the moon came down and said, "Illumination."
The pool stood still, but I think earth hovered under Raven,
and on the path the signs of love and crossing.

VII.

Laughing and crying, twin meets at the crossing twin.
They do not ask the mirror. Gold licks of illumination.
Eden smells of cedar. Raven holds his wings and sucks his stone.

Dreams and the Common Good

COMPOSED LIKE THEM

November 11, 1978

A pair of strange old birds
flew right into my dream,
Orville's and Wilbur's crates
waking me up with a start,
knocking my ivory gate,
calling me up to see
some old-time movie I knew
I never wanted to be.
Out of my past they came
creaking above Pat Bay,
come from a small backyard
in Kitty Hawk, USA. Or come
from farther away. Come from
the Ancient of Days. Tacky
old spiritual pair,
idle, extinct, and adored.

Am I the one with wings
fixed on with faulty glue?
Or am I the angelic form
doting, unfaithful, and true?
No matter who I am,
I'm sure they're here to stay,
I swear their corruption's done,
their wings now silvery-grey;
moth-eaten skeletons,
odd awkwardness at play.

Out of the fire they came
into Comedic light,
dragonflight spheres of thought,
filigreed lace for my sight.
But living together so long,
aloft in the petalled night,
has muted their loon-like song
to which they had every right.

Is this what Auden knew,
that the pair are secretly bored,
cruising that River of Light,
scaring the illiterate horde?
Too old to mate, do they get
from Alighieri's shore
a voyeuristic view of this
small round polished floor
which makes us passionate,
or leaves us cold – and late?

A few feet above Pat Bay,
dear lovers, you float upon
my childhood's airforce base,
my obsolescent song.
Old combatants up there,
hang-gliding Gemini,
yet sombre, home at last,
mechanically free,
steering your time machine
all for the likes of me.

I the dreamer dream
this flight at 51,
I, astonished and awed
under the moon and sun;
I, under the supernova,
asleep on the small round floor,
hear cackles of Zennish laughter
riming ecstatic puns.
I with my *Vita Nova*,
I with my lines undone.

LINES FROM GWEN. LINES FOR BEN.

1, 3, 5, 7

Who is this woman I know only slightly,
  Gwendolyn MacEwen, looking down at her notebook,
self-possessed, dressed in a dress, looking like
Gwendolyn MacEwen, poet, Egypt's fabulist, coolly writing
  as I watch her from the dream

1, 3, 5, 7

I am in the heat of childbirth
Her poem announces her as if I didn't matter:

1, 3, 5, 7

she writes again, breathing
evenly un/natural in the heat of odd numbers, out in the cold.

What was I am asking antecedent to the critical delirium
of love that did not give birth? Why what I am asking I
pushed out was only the idiot addition of one and one make two?

She stares from her distance

Why was it we who were magic animals could not fit into
poems and be happy? What was I am asking required of us
beyond cages we carried in case?

Four-footed now Cartesian daylight's nominal dumb ceremonial

Evens at Odds

She stares from her distance
  as if we didn't matter

I am in the heat of ...

O

add Origin, music the 1, 3, 5, 7, equalling 16

even dreams
        four / fours
                night's numinous quaternity.

Love four years only hyperventilating four fears I
owe you for what?

Blossoms.

Gwendolyn was writing in the dream
        I am in the heat of childbirth

she at her standing desk self-possessed
           1, 3, 5, 7
she wrote again and split

        as I woke
            without a word

METAPHYSICS OF SPRING

Blossoms –
powder of pink
moths, sift
of mystic wind-
watchers
shift of desire's
bled light
gloss of – ah, gross
matter (great
matter), it does
not, even
matter
burning / the
shudder of / in
the wing's!
in shell's pink
growing, birth
of the world
/ feathery
flesh or love
what matter?

ESCHATOLOGY OF SPRING

Death, Judgment, Heaven, Hell,
and Spring. The Five Last Things,
the least of which I am, being in
the azaleas and dog-toothed violets
of the South of Canada. Do not tell me
this is a cold country. I am also in
the camellias and camas of early, of
abrupt birth.
We are shooting up for the bloody
judgment of the six o'clock news.
Quick, cut us out from the deadlines
of rotting newspapers, quick, for the
tiny skeletons and bulbs will tell you
how death grows and grows in Chile and
Chad. Quick, for the small bones pinch
me and insects divulge occult excrement
in the service of my hyacinth, my trailing
begonia. And if you catch me resting
beside the stream, sighing against
the headlines of this pastoral, take
up your gun, the flowers blossoming
from its barrel, and join this grief, this
grief: that there are lambs, elegant black-
footed lambs in this island's eschatology,
Beloved.

SPRING THING

OK. It's all right with me
    if you insist on repeating yourself.
        I do that too, but the wonder

is in small change.
    I'll give you three lines
        for a new strategy to set things straight:

You were always phenomenal
    epiphenomenal – and blind.
        Open my eyes, lidded with this slow snow.

THE DAYS OF THE UNICORNS

    I remember when the unicorns
roved in herds through the meadow
behind the cabin, and how they would
lately pause, tilting their jewelled
horns to the falling sun as we shared
the tensions of private property
and the need to be alone.

Or as we walked along the beach
a solitary delicate beast
might follow on his soft paws
until we turned and spoke the words
to console him.

It seemed they were always near
ready to show their eyes and stare
us down, standing in their creamy
skins, pink tongues out
for our benevolence.

As if they knew that always beyond
and beyond the ladies were weaving them
into their spider looms.

I knew where they slept
and how the grass was bent
by their own wilderness
and I pitied them.

It was only yesterday, or seems
like only yesterday when we could
touch and turn and they came
perfectly real into our fictions.
But they moved on with the courtly sun
grazing peacefully beyond the story
horns lowering and lifting and
lowering.

I know this is scarcely credible now
as we cabin ourselves in cold
and the motions of panic
and our cells destroy each other
performing music and extinction
and the great dreams pass on
to the common good.

Poems of Failure I. *The Empire City*, a novel by Paul Goodman, was the beginning of my interest in anarchism. The "little lady" (who could levitate) and the "Flying Dutchman" are both characters in the novel. The quotations at the end of this section are from Part 3, Ch. 12, "The Dead of Spring." (*The Empire City*, Indianapolis: Bobbs-Merrill, 1959).

II. Two basic works on the life of Kropotkin are *Memoirs of a Revolutionist* by Peter Kropotkin, ed. James Allen Rogers (Gloucester, MA: Peter Smith, [1962] 1967), and *The Anarchist Prince* by George Woodcock and Ivan Avakumović (London / New York: T.V. Boardman, 1950). Kropotkin was, among many other things, a gifted geographer and explorer with particular interest in eastern Siberia. "Poems of Failure," II and III, telescope some of the major events in his life.

III. The quotation at the end of the poem is from *The Letters of Sacco and Vanzetti*, ed. Marion D. Frankfurter and Gardner Jackson (New York: E.P. Dutton, 1960).

VI. I am not sure of the significance of the dream words "Russia, 1965."

Socrates is based mainly on Plato's *Phaedo*.

Kropotkin Dmitrov: a small town outside Moscow where Kropotkin died, February 8, 1921.

Still There Are Wars ... A sound poem to be chanted.

A Question of Questions, V. "If the dominant phantasy in this particular group was that the therapist had 'the answer' and that if they could get 'the answer' they would not be suffering, the therapist's task, like a Zen Master's, is to point out that their suffering is not due to their getting 'the answer' from him, but is in the state of desire they are in, whereby they posit the existence of 'an answer' and are frustrated because they do not seem to be getting it." I am indebted to R.D. Laing (*The Self and Others*, London: Tavistock, 1961, p. 114) for the inspiration for this poem – as well as the red-crested woodpecker. The description of *Dryocopus pileatus* comes from Roger Tory Peterson's *Field Guide to Western Birds*, 2nd ed. (Boston: Houghton-Mifflin, 1961).

Wilson's Bowl My friendship with Lilo Berliner sprang out of our mutual interest in petroglyphs – First Nation rock carvings. Before she committed suicide she left her letters from the noted anthropologist, Wilson Duff, on my doorstep. Their correspondence had a peculiar intimacy, perhaps made possible by the fact that they never met. These poems are my attempt to deal with Lilo's obsessions and death.

Found Poem This poem was found in "Theory and Function of the *Duende*" by Federico García Lorca, translated by J.L. Gili. In this essay Lorca explains how *Duende* is different from the non-Spanish Muse or Angel or Daemon. "The sense of the presence of death."

She Sings When Lilo discovered the petroglyph bowl near the house she rented from Beth and Ray Hill (*Indian Petroglyphs of the Pacific Northwest*, Saanichton, B.C.: Hancock House, 1974) on Salt Spring Island, she dedicated it to Wilson Duff (who had committed suicide a few months before in August, 1976) and named it "Wilson's Bowl."

The Place Is Where You Find It "Wild Woman" – First Nation mythological figure, Tsonoqua (now Dzunuk̲'wa), or "wild-woman-of-the-woods."

Twin Masks These stone masks were brought from Ottawa and Paris for *Images of Stone B.C.: Thirty Centuries of Northwest Coast Indian Sculpture*, an exhibition originating at the Art Gallery of Greater Victoria, organized by gallery director, Richard Simmons, and Wilson Duff. Lilo went to see the exhibition, both in Victoria and Vancouver, about five times. She was particularly moved by these masks, undoubtedly great works of art, as was I. There are various meanings given to twins in First Nation lore. The most apposite here is that "If twins grew up in the proximity of other people, the twins would die." (Wilson Duff, "The Upper Stalo Indians of the Fraser Valley, B.C.," *Anthropology in British Columbia*, Memoir No. 1, Victoria: B.C. Provincial Museum Department of Education, 1953).

Composed Like Them This poem arrived first as pure rhythm and metre, and though I disliked the movement I went with it to discover it was a rough parody of W.H. Auden's metre in "September 1, 1939." There are also references to Dante's *The Divine Comedy*, "*Paradiso*," *canto* XXII where the earth is seen by Dante and Beatrice from the eighth heaven as:

> *The small round floor which makes us passionate*
> *I, carried with the eternal Twins, discerned,*
> *From hill to harbour, plain to contemplate:*
> *Then to the beauteous eyes my eyes returned.*
> (trans. Laurence Binyon)

Lines from Gwen When one of the readers of the manuscript said she was unsure about "nominal dumb ceremonial," etc., I wrote, "Why are you unsure about 'nominal dumb ceremonial' and 'Origin'? The 'magic animals' are now only circus animals – or thinking therefore am-ing proper decorous statistical and formal. 'Origin' means go back to the beginning. Zero. O. Then add up the 1, 3, 5, 7 and get 16. But Origin as birth hole too, maybe, and beginning of sound, sight, etc."

The Days of the Unicorns "paws": dream overlap of lion and unicorn.

1984

Water and Light

GHAZALS AND ANTI GHAZALS

CONTENTS

(Quotations from *Ghazals of Ghalib*)

LIGHT   LIGHT   LIGHT   LIGHT
LIGHT   LIGHT   LIGHT   LIGHT

Old doom pining away
in forest's mossy undergrowth

WEARY   WEARY   WEARY   WEARY
Oh Lord Krishna DANCE

Shiva DANCE, your anklet bells
waking the waterlilies in the pool

WATER AND LIGHT   WATER AND LIGHT
and the grand dark attending

Sunday Water: Thirteen Anti Ghazals

for Michael Ondaatje who introduced me to ghazals
and for Frank Scott

These poems, composed between September 18 and November 29, 1981, were written on unlined file cards ($4'' \times 6''$ and $3'' \times 5''$), beginning as an exercise in the ghazal form and ending in a quiet storm of six on Sunday, November 29.

In the previous spring I had belatedly discovered the ghazals of John Thompson in *Stilt Jack*, published posthumously by Anansi in 1978. Knowing little more about this ancient Persian form than what Thompson had said in his preface, my plan was to write one a day, though I usually wrote more than one when I stayed with the discipline. The plan was interrupted for most of October and November. But as I learned more about ghazals, I saw I was actually defying some of the traditional rules, constraints, and pleasures laid down so long ago.

"Drunken and amatory" with a "clandestine order," the subject of the traditional ghazal was love, the Beloved representing not a particular woman but an idealized and universal image of Love. The couplets (usually a minimum of five) were totally unlike the conventional English couplet and were composed with an ear and an eye to music and song.

Mine tend toward the particular, the local, the dialectical, and private. There are even a few little jokes. Hence "anti ghazals." And yet in the end (though I hope to write more), Love returns to sit on her "throne of *accidie*," a mystical power intrudes, birds sing, a sitar is plucked, and the Third Eye, opal, opens,

— P.W.
Salt Spring Island, B.C.

I watch the pile of cards grow.
I semaphore for help (calling stone-dead John Thompson).

A mist in the harbour. Hydrangea blooms turn pink.
A game of badminton, *shuttlecock*, hitting at feathers!

My family is the circumstance I cannot dance with.
At Banff I danced in black, so crazy, the young man insisting.

Four or five couplets trying to dance
into Persia. Who dances in Persia now?

A magic carpet, a prayer mat, red.
A knocked-off head of somebody on his broken knees.

Heidegger, notes of music
in his name.

The rose blooms because it blooms in the trellis.
A scale of black death because a scale of black death.

Around me, little creakings
of the house. Day's end.

The universe opens. I close.
And open, just to surprise you.

Come loves, little sheep, into
the barricades of the Fall Fair.

Mrs. Olsson at 91 is slim and sprightly.
She still swims in the clamshell bay.

Around the corner, Robin hangs out big sheets
to hide her new added-on kitchen from the building inspector.

I fly from the wide-open mouth of the seraphim.
Something or somebody always wants to improve me.

Come down, eagle, from your nifty height.
Let me look you in the eye, Mr. America.

Crash – in the woods at night.
Only a dead tree falling.

Ten white blooms on the sundeck.
The bees have almost all left. It's September.

The women writers, their heads bent under the light,
work late at their kitchen tables.

Winter breathes in the wings of the last hummingbird.
I have lost my passion. I am Ms. Prufrock.

So. So. So. Ah – to have a name like *Wah*
when the deep purple falls.

And you have sent me a card
with a white peacock spreading its tail.

My morning poem destroyed by the good-neighbour policy.
Mrs. Olsson, organic gardener, lectures me on the good life.

Damned dark hole! Rabbit
in her rabbit warren, pushing them out.

Oh this *is* cozy, all of us together watching
the news, catching each other's tics and flickers.

The square ring on her third finger, six seed pearls.
On her right index finger, tiny diamond-shaped jade.

The grand design. The setting sun.
All the big animals turn toward the Great Wall of China.

Yahweh is a speckled bird pecking at tree bark.
We are the insects most excellent to his taste.

Scorpio with his secrets and his sting
is nobody's fool and nobody's following.

A song preserved from childhood, meadowlark's,
mocks faintly now from the nesting-fields of Lansdowne.

Muttering and casting about each morning
for the secret heart of a poem.

The eggs of Yahweh crack in the tight nest.
Too big his bright wings. Too heavy his warm breast.

Evening autumn closes in. African marigolds
shine on. Harvest moons.

Land's End. I don't believe it. Down there –
among the reeds: cities of light and water.

From Russia, three embroidered velvet hats.
A balalaika. A necklace of amber beads.

The wood still has to be split, but I am off
again, into the air, flying East

with poems *From the Country of Eight Islands*. Hokku.
Haiku. Chōka. Kanshi. Kouta. Tanka. Renga. *Seeds*.

The flow, flux, even the effluent stormy
in high wind, dashing into the poison mind.

Trees downed by a gale. Sea-wrack matting
the shore, the morning after. The wind said,

Take that, and that! and that! continuing
on its path with the same message for inlanders stranded.

Pathetic fallacies deep in these bones.
Pathetic oneness with weathers and cosmic dust.

Pretty pebble, divine bird, honourable tree –
all in me. Take this, and this, and this – in memory of.

My loves are dying. Or is it that my love
is dying, day by day, brief life, brief candle,

a flame, *flambeau*, torch, alive, singing
somewhere in the shadow: Here, this way, here.

Hear the atoms ambling, the genes a-tick
in grandfather's clock, in the old bones of beach.

Sun on the Sunday water in November.
Dead leaves on wet ground. The ferry leaves on time.

Time in your flight – O – a wristwatch strapped
to my heart, ticking erratically, winding down.

The pull, this way and that, ultimately into the pull
of the pen across the page.

Sniffing for poems, the forward memory
of hand beyond the grasp.

Not grasping, not at all. *Reaching* is
different – can't touch that sun.

Too hot. That star. This cross-eyed
vision. Days and nights, sun, moon – the up-there claptrap.

And down here, trappings of "as above" – crosswalks,
traffic lights, sirens, this alexandrite burning on this hand.

Tuned lyre (lyrebird, myna,
parrot, parakeet, peacock) paradox –

not musical, though the brilliant plumage
variegated for those who do not

sing well, screech, shriek, scream
in the jungle trees – the *ee* sounds

unlyrical plumage, especially with *S*'s.
On the other hand (plucked), sea, see,

or me, thee, three in the thicket,
perfectly musical

and coloured enough, though featherless,
for a kind of flying.

Drunken and amatory, illogical, stoned, mellifluous
journey of the ten lines.

The singer sings one couplet or two
over and over to the Beloved who reigns

on the throne of *accidie*, distant, alone,
hearing, as if from a distance, a bell

and not this stringy instrument scraping away,
whining about love's ultimate perfection.

Wait! Everything is waiting for a condition of grace:
the string of the Sitar, this Gat, a distant bell,

even the Beloved in her bored flesh.

The card is dealt, out of the blank pack,
preordained, imprinted on inner eye.

Now for the Third Eye to read the grown signs:
flickers of doubt tic mouth, twitch eye's lid.

But it's open – always – the third one,
guardian of splendours, crimes.

Seeing all, all-seeing, even in sleep knows
space (outer, inner, around), tracks freak snows,

slumbering ponies. Love, I am timid
before this oracular seer, opal, apple of my eye.

The Birds

Yoko Ono was seen in the Empress Hotel today.
She can never be seen for herself alone again.

Shots ring out in Iran, Afghanistan,
El Salvador.

At night here pitlampers
kill deer.

Everywhere the killings go on.
In my own hand a flea died only yesterday.

I sit in my quilted jacket calling the birds
whose warning cries strike just beyond the window.

My dear ladies, birds of a feather,
the astounding patience of your hatching.

Your little eggs drop into the thatched nest
just like that – *phlup, phlup, phlup* –

speckled, tinted, and, within, miniatures
of your own birdiness held in suspension.

Chirp, chirp and trill, Yes, as the acid
rain falls on your Easter feathers you

puff up. Ladies, ladies, how you confound me

with your embroidered eyes, your faithful smiles
your dear familiar songs.

for Mary Melfi

I'd never hate to see flamingos
walking out of the mango patch.

What should I tell her who can see
in the mirror the chance of a bird

standing on one pink leg? Tell her
to shut her eyes tight, boil her ears

in essence of camellias, turn herself
over to the green haunt orchid

on the next blue Monday?
Why should I tell her anything?

She's the Queen holding a mummified cat.

Grey-eyed dryad, have you seen one
if only for the sound of

grey-eyed dryad. Or gull gone
into blue empyrean, the lift

of wind fabulous, flowing, free-for-all.
Nothing is pure praxis,

axis of this globe sends
degree by degree us into curved

path of portent, accident, perishable
eye-sad dryad. Look at her. Here.

The varied thrush, the orchard oriole,
the crying dove, the skin-smooth olive

green, olive-green, with a red
pimiento

heart.

Peacock blue. Words fail me,
Fishstar, for the packed, inbred

splendour of this bird. His strut,
the cock of his head, a royal courtier

in the barnyard. Essex. See how the
Fabulous points into the spectrum, pecks out

accurately a blue-green scream for Elizabeth.
It is morning. It is the first morning

of creation, an absurd idea, but I tell you,
Fishstar, the colour of chaos was not

Peacock blue.

Brightness burns off the coal-black
shimmering brats of the branch

The common crow, ill-tempered and always hungry
infested with matter

shooting out flares from your winter gangland
bouncing the bough with *harrumphs.*

Incendiaries of the Bad News
You flaming newsprint!

What do you mean in this religious dark
damning me with feathers and your hot light?

Four swans in Fulford Harbour
thirty on Somenos Lake.

Wings, uprush of inspiration, brush
past the broken shell of my ear.

In bodies of water and air
ructions, lacunae.

A green canary breasts round her nest
claws footholding the world.

Sweep this away. The clean sweep.
Angelus ringing, spare-hearted gong.

I Daniel

for Timothy Findley

I.

But I Daniel was grieved
and the vision of my head troubled me,

and I do not want to keep
the matter in my heart

for the heart of the matter
is something different.

Neither do I want happiness
without vision.

I am apocryphal and received.
I live now and in time past

among all kinds of musick – sackbut,
cornet, flute, psaltery, harp, and dulcimer.

You come bearing jobs and treachery and money,

but I Daniel, servant to powers
that pass all understanding,

grieve into time, times, and the dividing of time.

II.

I also serve the kings,
but my own name fascinates me

with its slippery syllables.
I live in a mysterious book;

my imitators incline me to derision
for they too are fascinated by my name,

by the flagrant musick of the old lore,
sackbut and psaltery, by the grief

in all my actions.

III.

The coin is dropped into my palm.
I become the messenger, see –

here, now, in my own hand
the printout of the King's text

which he has forgotten
and I remember.

Listen, I dream the dream,
I deliver its coded message

and pocket the coin.
Keep your jobs and dollars.

I go into the dark on the King's business
and spend my time thanking him

for the privilege of my servitude.

IV.

The musick of the dulcimer was a silver bird
flying about my ears

when I closed my eyes and sealed them.
Nebuchadnezzar

tapped me on the shoulder
after I'd done the job;

but all I could hear was bird
song in the apparatus,

all I could hear were three notes
from the string of the dulcimer

and one on the cornet.

V.

I ate no pleasant bread. The fast
unbroken for weeks,

then I Daniel looked and saw –
but what do you care for the grief

of what I Daniel understood by
books the number of the years of desolation?

Confusion of faces, yours among them,
the poetry tangled, no vision of my own to speak of.

The hand moved along the wall.
I was able to read, that's all.

VI.

I, even I Daniel, whose countenance
changed, said nothing about a broken heart.

Always it was the dangerous ones
who needed me

in the garden, under the stars –
always I found what they needed

flat on my face in a deep sleep:
"Messenger, here is your message."

And I Daniel fainted
and was sick certain days.

VII.

In those days I Daniel
was mourning three full weeks.

Haunted by numbers: what "passed seven
times," and what "shall be for a time,

and times, and a half"? Four horns or one
or one becoming four in the breakdown

of the bicameral mind – wherein I Daniel
alone saw the vision –

VIII.

It was only politics, wars and rumours,
in the vision or dream:

four beasts of terror with their
numbers game. I play and trick my way

out of this scene into the arms of Gabriel
who does not hear the tune performed

on sackbut, psaltery, harp and dulcimer.

Frivolities

for Connie Rooke

Mulberry tree with innocent eyes,
Catalpa with your huge hands,

I am looking at you
so why can't you look back?

Seduce me, Mulberry, with your silk-spun eyelashes,
applaud, Catalpa, with leafy ambuscades.

I am a patient person from time to time,
willingly would I fall into your entrapments

of silk stockings and flowery candelabra.
Or should I save myself with long voyages

interstellar longings
where we might meet as pure event

and I would say Mulberry tree, Catalpa,
and you would say, simply, Phyllis.

My soul, my soul, who said that?
as the rain stumbles over my mental horizon

horizon which wavers, creates the mirage
of a café in Milano where

Mary, he says, what shall we do tonight?

Tonight, tonight, love, what shall we do tonight?
The mirage settles into rain falling

into the harbour and onto the day I own
feeding the heat of dry September

September and the cats restless, hungry
in view of winter, in view of cold

cold as the curse of mere matter, *Mère*
matter, the subject family, the repeated

word ready to pounce out of the thunder
out of the rainforest where leap the wild, bereft deer.

Is there such a thing as a vulgar plant?
Oh amaryllis, out of Africa, forgive me.

Will the haiku butterfly decorously
settle on the bronze bell?

Whose song is this anyway?
Is it a song being sung

on the narrow road to the North?
Oh *Fishstar*!

The cabbage moth looks innocent
on the green leaf. Kiss, kiss.

These lines are also hungry
biting a hole in the yellow paper

on which Fishstar writes.

A lozenge of dream
sticks on my tongue

Soulange, Stonehenge
sugar mite, maple –

a candy poem
slips down my throat

a green droplet
a sweet mantra

Dentelle, she-teeth, milk-tooth,
a mouthful of lace.

Cobwebs with the devil's ace,
cut tooth, cuttlefish, scrimshaw.

You there, you too were only a piece
of string in the needle's eye, once,

now frantic, idle in the sun, a great
cobweb strung across your mind:

you spin it out, saliva and
heart's beat battering the great

hole of emptiness in space –
somewhere – in lachrymose

galaxies crying for their done,
banged-in stars.

Reserved books. Reserved land. Reserved flight.
And still property is theft.

Guilt in the morning and afternoon.
Stick-pin doll, that's me, needled.

Night-time rattle of bones. Island
a midden, old shells, old pots, old combs.

Inside this skull an oyster brain.
Pearl / plain. Pearl / plain. Earth works.

The purple orchid he brought me
to wear at my reading

lies face up in the blue-glazed bowl –
a Ladyslipper with several eyes.

They stare and stare. I hear, strangely,
the music of Vivaldi's Concerto for Three

Violins in the falling dusk. Poems
of many scents and various hues beguile me.

Once in the early dawn of my childhood
I stood in a garden and saw the Queen of the Fairies

step on a single drop of dew.

QIAN: MODESTY: *Respectful, humble, yielding, retiring*
     25th day of the 12th moon, January 27–February 1, 1984.

Be still and move with the Tao:
Society has rules of decorum.

Helpers must be modest
and realize their function.

If one does well
one should expect praise.

She swings in her hammock
memorizing the laws of physics.

Pudeur. Caution protects
rightness. In her mind

('s eye) she prowls the aisles of Safeway
past pomegranates, kiwi fruit, mangoes,

limes, past babies in snugglies.
She swings, she sniffs the air, curls

her toes in strings of the white cotton
hammock,

rests in the Tao, moves with it,
trails fingers through pale lakes of air

humbly. Assents to the curve of time –
its modest wish –

sucking a tangerine, yielding sweetly
to shy, succulent (tenured) Professor Death.

January 28, 1984

Middle Distance

History and secrecy – that's what I said
as a member of a panel whose topic was

Why Poetry? And why not, I asked,
my right brain humming sedition.

Patrick insisted on games and the nature
of games. Gary agreed with the seriousness

and playfulness of that. And Tom, who
started it all, was concerned about the

alienation of the young, whom he loves.
We were all uncomfortable and knew we were failures.

The man from Iraq in the audience said,
"Where I come from when you fill out a job

application you begin by quoting poetry
and when you flirt you quote poetry

and when you marry poetry is all around you.
Why don't you speak of feelings!"

And when you die at the executioner's hands
(he did not say this though most of his family

was murdered) do you also quote poems, Amin?
Oh Allah. Why not?

Oh You who keep disappearing
behind a black cloud like a woman

behind her veil, how do you feel
shut off like that from the perfect

obedience of your worshippers?
There is this Mirror, clear and unchanging?

There is this Poet counting his syllables;
he is planting lilies and roses

in cracks of the universe. He tells how
the Mirror clouds up in the heat

of his rhymes, how he goes
crazy in your black weather.

The Authors are in Eternity,
or so Blake said,

but I am here, feet planted
on the ground;

I am listening to the song
of the underground river.

I go down to the same river twice,
remembering, always remembering.

I am you in your jewel-domed reading room,
I am you in your kayak skimming.

I stand in one place risking almost everything.
I weep for the last notes.

The river stones are polished
by the blue-veined hands of Ishtar.

Poor Fishstar! Yet – all is not lost.

LEANING

I am half-way up the stairs
of the Leaning Tower of Pisa.

Don't go down. You are in this
with me too.

I am leaning out of the Leaning
Tower heading into the middle distance

where a fur-blue star contracts, becomes
the ice pond Brueghel's figures are skating on.

North Magnetic pulls me like a flower
out of the perpendicular

angles me into outer space
an inch at a time, the slouch

of the ground, do you hear that?
the hiccup of the sludge about the stone.

(Rodin in Paris, his amanuensis, a torso ...)
I must change my life or crunch

over in vertigo, hands
bloodying the inside tower walls

lichen and dirt under the fingernails
Parsifal vocalizing in the crazy night

my sick head on the table where I write
slumped one degree from the horizontal

the whole culture leaning ...

the phalloi of Miës, Columbus returning
stars all shot out –

And now this. Smelly tourists
shuffling around my ears

climbing into the curvature.
They have paid good lira to get in here.

So have I. So did Einstein and Bohr.
Why should we ever come down, ever?

And you, are you still here

tilting in this stranded ark
blind and seeing in the dark.

Ah Ghalib, you are drinking too much,
your lines are becoming maudlin.

Here, take this tea and sober up. The moon
is full tonight, and I can't sleep.

And look – this small branch of cherry
blossoms, picked today, and it's only February.

You could use a few cool Japanese images
to put you on the straight and narrow.

Still, I love to study your graceful script,
Urdu amorous, flowing across the page.

There were nights I watched you dip your pen
into the old Persian too, inscribe "Asad"

with a youthful flourish. Remember Asad,
Ghalib?

Mirza Asadullah Beg Khan, who are you really?
Born in Agra, of Turkish ancestry,

fond of women, politics, money, wine.
"Losses and consequent grief" a recurring

theme, also "a poetry ... of what was,
what could have been possible."

Ah Ghalib, you are almost asleep,
head on the table, hand flung out,

upturned. In the blue and white jar
a cherry branch, dark pink in moonlight –

from the land of
only what is.

Hanging Fire

in memory of the poets
Gwendolyn MacEwen, bpNichol,
Bronwen Wallace

in poetry … sound will initiate thought by a process
of association. words call each other up, evoke
each other, provoke each other, nudge each other
into utterance … a form of thought that is not
rational but erotic because it works by attraction.
a drawing, a pulling toward. a "liking."

—Daphne Marlatt
musing with mothertongue

Titles of poems in quotation marks are "given" words,
phrases, or sentences that arrive unbidden in my head.
I've been tracking them for some time to see if there
are hidden themes, connections, a sub-rational
rationale. It seems there are.

—P.W.

Tour de Force

The arrogance. The above it all.
Ministrations of angels,
little holy ghosts fiddling
while the planets burn, sing.
For instance, superstrings,
immense smallness of, tangled
spaghetti, the metaphor
materializing unimaginable
piquant sauce, restores us
to middling size, for comparison:
minute white floss on the rose-
mary plant, one flower in bloom
of Queen Anne's lace.

Or shady dealings in the lab.
A handmade mouse with cancer
for generations, patented,
marketed, sold, as transgenic
engineering steers us to the
unity of all things.

I put my foot down on
such nonsense, trinkets of ever-
lasting gloom, animal suffering.
If I tangle with invisible
superstrings, hung up on
supergravity, elegant
mathematics, all this
weighty knowledge ...

"KRAKATOA" AND "SPIRITUAL STORM"

for Dorothy Livesay and bill bissett

Hot magma
        indigo dawn
wild yelps
        of pure physics
crack open deep sea
buttocks thrust up love lava
world heart / broken / cardiac
arrest.
Krakatoa. Krakatau.

The small gods gather
for countdown, each lifts
a finger to the wind (quake,
tide, tsunami) tastes
the cost of all-paroxysmal
sexual storm, lid blown off,
creator creating, a whim,
wham of blowup on shores –
Java, Sumatra, Hawaii –
blasting away 2,200 miles heard,
Krakatoan wind circling the dust
up high enough. Radiant

marvellous sunsets for years.
Spectacle. Le monocle de mon
oncle sent flying into the eye
of the storm (*spiritual* for him,
timbre just right, *pinhead*).

God, how I suffer to get this down as if I'd
been there watching the lava hit and run after
dogs and children and hens, cone island collapsing
into the sea. Always this me. Tourist, backpacked,
camera at ready, lens cap removed.

And the big gods come, finally, to the Pacific
for 36,000 dead, fallout, cinders, oracular
birth of Anak (child of) Krakatoa. Bad mouth.
Ash. Devolution. Darkness at noon.

So be it. So it was: May 20, 1883, "paroxysmal"
blast August 26, "climax" eruption August 27,
10 a.m. Masses of floating pumice near the
volcano so thick as to halt ships. Surrounding
region in darkness two and a half days.
Temperature worldwide lowered 0.27°.
Plant and animal life gone five years.
Anak (child of) Krakatoa active into
the 1980s.

Genetic spleen

Time lapse backwards

Mortal fear
Cassandra
Nostradamus
"Sons of guns"

I cannot surprise you. Not with the blue jay's
return. Not with the velvet yellow of pansyface,
not with my held-back fire. Apocalypse. Every-
thing predictable in the book. Ominous ocean.
Glacier waterslide. Occult fecal blood's old
testament. Rotted bodies. Sun's eclipse,
Venus swinging below the moon.

Veracity. Storm, calm, dilemmas, ditch-jumps.
Capacity for wonder. The spring of the mouse-
trap sprung, we are caught – thus and so – in
this pose, shadowed beyond doubt. Fire hanging
back for a more effective, filmic test site,
for desert bloom.

"MIASMA"

Stunned by the blow
                    polluting exhalations
poisonous effluvium
(infectious, noxious) putrid
matter and such a lovely
sound / word I hear "mimosa"
hidden there, the daze
the out-and-out sunshine yellow
of delirium, fever, malarial
swamp garden.
How the mind doth know
its own dictionary. Ditch-
water / standing water
still reflecting a bullrush,
calf, dragonfly, echo of
plasma, old hoedown
razzmatazz of this affliction.
Gearlock, warlock,
critter of the moon.

Between rosy dawn and the fifth dimension, the Morning Star shrugs and staggers off stage-right. But the flight's on time, sparks spackle the skyway with interludes of starling song. Trills, *pianissimo*, thunder above, Crimean surgery explores the lower gut, salvation at the edge of a blade, a summer of Sundays. Hah. One foot's through a place called EXIT, the other aboard sky-surfing nebulae. Vasty undertakings. Godawful daily grind.

Slippages, repeat performance, soundings profounder as down we go for the third time through green waters, pearl diving, operatic; or dead poets brought back on their knees second time around, garter snakes splitting through mind burn, matter disorders. Ho Hum. Jumping bugs. What a parade of fancy-frees, scared shitless half the time, sorrowing saints, dumb pets waiting for the can to open. *Bird brains, eagle eyes, sad sacks,* whose minds float on forgetfulness – to quartz, sapphire, topaz, emerald-hard memory shards, spooky auditions, Toad of Toad Hall greeting his guests at the door with his white butler's gloves on.

Blasé, having seen it all before blaze forth, "shook foil" or fingerprint, a big toe pronged, little one cracked on a hub. Whimsy, shenanigans, Irish clowns, Irish poets mad, like me, murderous Othellos, Pagliaccis. Oh, I would sing if I had a mind to, but I don't have the heart in images' aftersnow, in "in memoriams," Istanbul's still a thong away, but in that Paris café the waiter came hungry for kisses. Garçon!

Objects from the past   eye patch   or   eye catch mesmerism   tick-tock of waitings   arrivals so-longs   too many rushes of Pennsylvania (where she's never been) Pilgrim Fathers sad in their black brigades   the old found land   the far countree

Hot pursuit, or languorous. We are in. A blue lagoon
bird stands on one pale leg, a picture of reflection,
nothing ruffled. Waters lap, ingenious insects walk
on water; thoughts bloom like algae, fluorescent,
many-celled, liberated and dying in their own element.

* * *

The syntax of deep structure composes on the harp,
strings along.

* * *

Red hot spikes. Fire-walking.

* * *

Cadence in scene, in the *seen*, seeking out pattern,
finding where the eye catches, heart hooks, tangible
order, a cadence. Tantrums of tears at such pure
spirit, radiant things, on which the eyes close.

* * *

"Mind is shapely, Art is shapely." Ginsbergian insight,
Allen afloat on his untidy chaos, his good humours. Ahoy!

* * *

Fragmentation: to understand the parts, reify certain
curious particulars to our habit of framing.
(Management techniques – precious jewels in the Swiss
    watch,
the Cretaceous period slotted between Jurassic and
Cenozoic. See chart under GEOLOGY. See geology under
the chart.)

* * *

Some of it makes sense, shape, meaning meandering
river of biologic "soup" on which fish, birds, insects
feed, that feed us. River on which we move undulant,
forsaking all else for this infectious cruise.

"CORNFLOWERS & SAFFRON ROBES BELITTLE THE EFFORT"

Ssh, sigh, silence is coming, the night time blues. Hark. Ahem. Sir? I lift my arm, the wind chimes through my holy raiment. Mesmeric bells reduce the flies to slumber. Pajama party. The end of the Raj.

"SELF CITY"

Tram tracks, Metro, torso
junction; gunshots, expectorations,
bird twitter; eternal castle
on the hill,
passages, narrow, through
the problematics.

I speak, therefore I am,
or so I say, seeing
the egoless Transcendent
poised on the parapet,
armed & dangerous.

Bed-sitter, rock-bottom,
urban clutter.
Words. Words
jumping the gun
on soundlessness.
The river flows on,
of course, vile stream
of ever-exchanging platitudes.

a needle in a haystack
as rare as hens' teeth
a nose for news pushing
the fallen leaves back
for luscious worms
composted cash.
Ai! Ai!
I've fallen over again
into *despond*, occluded
rage, I tear up another
page of *Pilgrim's Progress*
I lie on Donne's love's
violet bank, say nothing
all the day, nothing into
the cliché-ridden night.
Pray you, undo this button.
Show me one hen's tooth.
I'll find the needle.
Thread it.

Migraine, on the sinistral,
right brain hammering left.
Bad science. Bad faith.
It's been a long time,
one outgrows them, they say.
But today.
Writhings, rage clenches
my fist. Frozen pea bag
smashes against the hearth.
Tears on the crocodile
pillow. Housebound.
Inwardbound. Pacing.
The wall-to-wall carpet
raises its ugly head
accosts my dead languages.
Wait for the pills to take:
heightened consciousness,
intense forms. Purple iris
astonishing after rain,
June greens green, greener.
My face? It too articulates
each muscle into word-spasms,
syllable kicks. Three poems
in one day. Breathing fire.
Swallowing hard. Arrogant
sentence fragments. *Can't*
get out.

"COMPENDIUM"

The weight of the world, Atlas,
or you, whoever you are, it's
the way our lives hang in the
balance, it's two-for-the-price-
of-one, Mao's Little Red Book,
the Home Hardware flyer, it's
frozen tears stashed on the
bathroom shelf.
Hanging together, we speak
volumes. Spoke.

Flutter of eyelash, mirror of rabbit's sick eyes. Experimental pain, gate lock on all that expression. Exploring the good old times, mascara, seduction, sex ploys. What you have to know is the technical procedure: implantation of dyes, location of cornea. *Loco. Loco.* The cries of the animals for "human interest" in my friend's continuing pain – his hearing those cries in the worst nights, his blessing of the animals, two by two.

That Flying Dutchman's caught on his own windmill
puffs himself up with genuine ether laughter. Around
and about wind plays tricks and suddens, scoops a paw
into the local topsoil, nothing here, nothing to do, alas.

"THE SALT TAX"

SATYA-GRA-HA. SATYA-GRA-HA. I never saw the MOO-VEE-VEE-VEE-VEE or the OP-OP-OP-PERA (by Philip Glass) and at the age of three I could not, in 1930, have grasped the meaning of the salt tax-ax-ax-ax, but might have seen a pho-oh-toe of Gandhi in the newspaper (and the power of TROOTH, as children do), of the skinny old ma-ahn and his 78 followers trickling down 200 miles to the edge of the Arabian Sea at Dandi on the entrance to the Gulf of Cambay.

Today and yesterday and the day before, the sliding doors opened to let me (age 61) see him (age 61) again as a vision of sparse white cloth, and hear-ear-ear again "child's play," which is what he said walking 10 or 12 miles a day had been all the way from Ahmedabad.

Satya-gra-ha-ha-ha, he had written before the trek, seriously to Lord Irwin, "Take your own salary. It is over 21,000 ru-ooh-pees per month ... you are getting over 700 ru-ooh-ooh-pees a day, against India's average income of less than 7 annas [4 cents] per day (eh-eh-eh?). Thus you are getting over 5,000 times India's average in-come- come-come! On bended knee, I ask you to ponder over this phe-nom-e-non-non ..."

On bended knee? And they walked on over the strewn petals, the strewn leaves, cheered by many villagers, the salt of the EARTH-EARTH-EARTH, ON-ON

to the Arabian ocean's taste, of tears, sah-ah-tya-yah-yah-gra-ha-ha-ah – ah, beautiful grace as they bent down to steal a handful of FREE-EE-DOM.

Well, thank *you* very much. The indices prick up their
ears, they tabulate the prospects – quick, a hit of doc-
trine. The poem expands its chest, looks you straight in
the eye, knows you for who you pretend to be, says, The
game is up, Buster, let's get serious.

Instructions for the faint of heart

Turn the turtle over. Test its white stomach.
Find your island. Find the treasure.
Take short naps through the heat of the day.
Drink clean water only, if you can find it.
Build a wall – or not at all.
Lead your pretty shadow by the pretty hand.

Terrorist directives

Know the code.
Translate it into a foreign language. Any foreign language.

Memorize the Plan. Do not try to understand it.
Make a new plan. Make a list. A longer list.
Forget it.

Crash course in Chaos science; likewise Particle Physics.

Abscond with the Access to Information Act.
Advertise your whereabouts on national TV.

Call the hotline. Say you're on your way with a crack
death squad.

Say your Now-I-lay-me's.

Have a drink on me.

"THE WAY OF ALL FLESH"

flash – at the corner of the eye
(right corner, right eye). The car
has crashed at the bottom of the hill;
its motor purrs like a sick cat,
and you read this as contentment.

Hanging Fire

"HANGING FIRE"

Furioso, flame-eyed Flamenco, castanets' death
rattle.

Guru from the frozen North heats up shamanically,
her two big feet *Southbound*.

As lights go out, crisis of lambency.
"Dresden / China" – or thereabouts.

A curtain of fire drops over the overview,
glass-like substances, "fragments of quartz."

They leap and hang in the air. Firebugs.
Organic memory goes up in smoke.

Action. Smiling. Acidulous. Eating its heart out.

"IGNIS FATUUS"

Sunlight sprays through rain; wind tumbles surf,
globe of a morning moon glows down – here, where
we need all the light we can get.

*   *   *

As if by design, nets fail. Shellfish pinch the
bottom of the bay. Floods of power. Surges of
information.

*   *   *

"Manitou"

*   *   *

Alders, elders, birch trees on the road to
Moscow's airport.

*   *   *

Down at the beach at night, we poked the sea
with sticks, stirred up the   *
                            *   *

night-blooming phosphorous.

*   *   *

Ignis fatuus, foolish fire, jack-o'-lantern, will-
o'-the-wisp. Marsh light from decomposing matter.
Delusional systems. Us.

*   *   *

Heavyweight a
heavy wait for
that unbearable that
moment of being
a featherweight a
spin of spume
on a dark wave a
wave of the hand's
farewell into
freefold
mystical fire's
wild mandala –
orange and gold
amoeba-like edges
breathing and push-
ing in weight-
less and out
on wall (spurge
mustard seed
primula) violent
centre-spawn
marauding the doubt-
less dust-filled
last gasp
unbearable morning
light being
switchable on and

"YOU ARE NOWHERE"

in the work. The work is kin.
It's all in the family.

The old brain beats: Opera, Opus,
opulent film of disease, disaster

opening, closing on the one hand and
on the other, the jewels of dualism.

You are somewhere in the world
of "the fire next time."

I am trying to find you.
You are nowhere. Somewhere

in the spas of Romanian cures,
Islamic solutions –

or into a slow fade of alpha waves,
floats of lepidoptera –

for Salman Rushdie

hanging f   hanging f   hanging f   hanging f
    ire   ire   ire   ire

hanging f
            ear
    hanging f
                ear
    hanging f
                ear
hanging f
        ear

"LENIN SKATING"

pAtⁱN A patiner   patina^{the}S^{TARS}
p^A   PATINA patiner patina

                                        e^{un}
                                       e^r_{the}S^{TARS}
                                         t

        MoonLightIce

      t   S^A ^RS
       _HE _T

               at ¹⁵Y_E
                        _A
                  Sr

              heskates

ON THE FROZen volGA
      on the froZen Volga THE FROZEN VOLGA

        AT S^I^MB_IR
                   _R
               S_T
             _S   thebladescutcleanthrough
          E^R_U
    E   C I   the
     _R_O_T   f _u t^u r   E

                              e_r o^{se}_r o^{se}^r

         b^a l l_et   i ^chisfigures 888888ssss

  _T^HE T S A R ^S*
                          *****
                         ***   ** Ω
                          ***** ** Ω^ΩΩ Δ
                            ****   Ω_ΩΩ
                            ** Δ   μμμμμμμμμμ
   VLADIMIRVLADIMIR *   >>>>>>>>> <<<<<<<<
                                        ᵨᵨ
  <<<<<<<<<<<<<<<<<<<<<<<<<<<<<<<<<<<<<<< ᵨ^{ᵨᵨᵨᵨᵨᵨ}ᵨ>

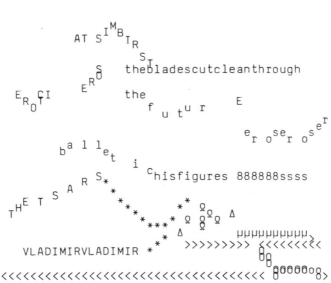

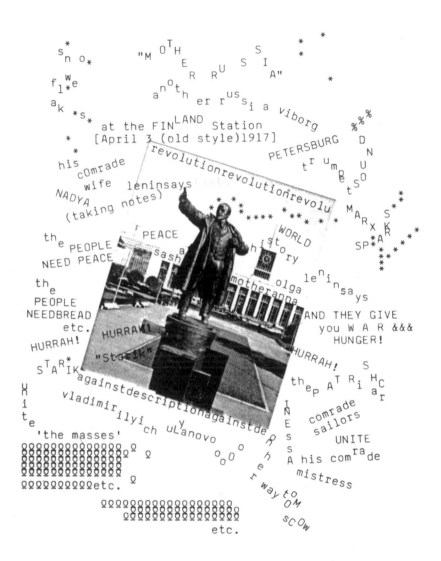

s   *   O T H   S   *   *
  n o*   "M   R   U   I   *
 w   E   R   S   A"
f e   a o   r   us
l *   th er r   si a viborg
a *s*   at the FIN^LAND Station   %%%
k   [April 3 (old style)1917]   D
   *   PETERSBURG   N U
his comrade revolutionrevolutionrevolu tr u m p e t S O
     wife leninsays   MARXSK
NADYA   SP*A R

(taking notes)

the PEOPLE   PEACE   WORLD
   NEED PEACE   sash a   history leninsays

the   motheranna olga
  PEOPLE
  NEEDBREAD   AND THEY GIVE
   etc.   you W A R &&&
  HURRAH! HURRAH!   HUNGER!
     "Starik"   HURRAH!   S
STARIK*   thePATRiarcH
    againstdescriptionagainstde   INE
W vladimirilyich uLanovo   y   S comrade
h   o   S sailors
i   'the masses'   o   A UNITE
t ΩΩΩΩΩΩΩΩΩΩΩΩΩ Ω   o   comrade
e ΩΩΩΩΩΩΩΩΩΩΩΩΩ   o   A his comrade
  ΩΩΩΩΩΩΩΩΩΩΩΩΩΩ Ω   mistress
  ΩΩΩΩΩΩΩΩΩΩΩetc. Ω   r way to
      ΩΩΩΩΩΩΩΩΩΩΩΩΩΩΩΩΩ   OM
          ΩΩΩΩΩΩΩΩΩΩΩΩΩΩΩ   sCOw
                etc.

June 25, 1989. Helsinki train station. I buy Kleenex, oranges, and *The Guardian* for the trip. I'm missing Bill and Tiff more now that the conference is over. This was to be the special "non-literary" part of the journey. But it's good to rest, be quiet after all that talk. I'm haunted by Lenin's ghost, the image of the sealed train. Why this obsession? The Romance of Revolution? The last agony of the Oedipus complex? The anxiety of (patriarchal) influence? The poem's pure, peculiar means and ends.

Gorky parked around the station seeing suspicious characters everywhere, then boarded the train. My new Finnish friends told me to head straight for the dining-car for caviar and vodka. But nyet. No caviar, no vodka, no sole amandine today. I watch as the train pulls past unmoving boxcars sprayed solid and lurid with graffiti, but what the words say I don't know. The countryside's sparse and lovely. I try to see it with Lenin's slanty eyes, blinking. Did it look very different in April 1917?

At the border, armed guards on the parapet. A long stop on both sides. I get my rubles, study the Russian alphabet, want to talk to the Japanese travellers, don't want to talk to anyone. Will the *Intourist* greeter be there at the station? Of course, and I'm hurried into a car and taken to the Moskva Hotel. It's all too speedy. I can't catch up with that old movie in my head.

Up Nevsky Prospekt in the just-past-midsummer night, feeling low. Everything dusty and crumbly in the heat wave. "I think, the poetry is / not the words." Barry McKinnon. He meant, I think, the melody lingers on. In *The Death of a Lyric Poet*. I turn back, it's too late.

June 26. Spectacular entrance into the dining room this morning – I slipped and fell with force, but no serious damage, except to my self-confidence. Touristy stuff today. Long walk exploring in the a.m., then the usual delays and hurdles to get the bus to Petrodvorets on the Gulf of Finland. Peter the Great's getaway, "Mon Plaisir." It is, it is. Inside jammed with sightseers, outside hot, easy, wild grasses, flowers, a trick fountain where kids and grown-ups play.

I still don't understand what was the inspiration to restore these old palaces and mansions of the aristocracy. Was it a prophetic vision of the tourism industry? Or the deep down *conservateur* instinct? Postwar delusions of grandeur, or make-work? There's more to it than just (just!) the "People's palaces."

I've planned to meet R. outside the hotel (Soviet citizens are not supposed to enter these tourist domains). I'd sent a photo so he recognizes me, we take a cab, he insists on paying. As we enter the scruffy elevator in the highrise, he calls the building a slum, the beginning of the revelations of their unhappiness. I tell him it could be Toronto or New York. A real Russian welcome, even a big cake. I've brought a few gifts – CDs, a book on UFOs, pantyhose for L. And vodka. R. demonstrates his superb sound system, too loud for me. They complain about shortages, everything's worse, their disillusionment. Their son wants to be a drummer in a jazz band, says he hates anti-Semites, repeats passionately he hates anti-Semites, he's "one-quarter Jewish," they still want out.

We watch a popular satiric TV news program during which (R. translates) the day's haul at the jail is reviewed. A young man has been arrested because he did a take-off in a public place of the famous Lenin pose: one arm out in orating fashion, one hand tucked into the vest, as in the statue at the Finland Station. When asked by the interviewer why he did it, "for the hell of it," he says. The power of parody. I forgot to ask if he also did the speech, "The people need bread ..."

I love the ride through the Leningrad night in the taxi, elated by my visit to their home. This would not have been possible in 1967 when we first met. Contingency.

June 27. The Hermitage today where I lose my tour group at just the right moment – on my way to the Impressionist collection. Then, later, I have to hurry to find my way back to the bus, parked on the far side of the huge square. Flashes of Tiananmen, flashes of here, the Tsars' old palace guards, the troops, the "clashes."

In the evening I have a drink, new to me, Bitter Cinzano, at the hotel bar with a woman cellist from the U.S. She talks a lot about her jewels. It's still light, so we take a stroll in the park-cemetery across the way. Poets' graves with real and plastic flowers, some old dusty down-and-outers, and young guys trying to do a blackmarket currency deal. Can't get a line by Odysseas Elytis out of my head: "All of us with eaten faces will return some day from the Truth-sites."

Tomorrow – back to the Hermitage, back to Helsinki, back to the Finland Station.

"PASSACAGLIA"

The poet dives off the deep end
of the lyric poem to surface on
Nevsky Prospekt in Leningrad
on a hot June night
missing her friends who ought
to be here in the hot night
walking up Nevsky Prospekt
she has broken her habit of
repetition, the snowdrops,
the snowdrops, the snowdrops
in the white nights, white
nights, white nights, the
death of the lyric poem
the death –

Long suffering is active, alive with plenipotentiaries of
the dead and gone, the lingering on of the living, long
strolling afternoons of carry-me-forward to darkness.
But first the sun goes down in plumes. Come. The
hand-in-hand – *a failure of will, a stumbling* –

*   *   *

Say it again, *"The Years,"* the art of fiction, the art of
pleasing, pleasures of pain. Or HEAD-ON: strike, revolu-
tion, power overthrown and not overthrown. Burned out
of her home again, she carries the flame. Oppressive
regime. Corruption. Gorge rises on clips of language,
clips of film. No news is bad news. Those who lie slain.

*   *   *

Tame my heart, featherbrain, you who are not tamed
squawk and feed your young, and then you leave them
hungry to flop up the cedar bough, sway, test wormy
freedom with a lift of small wings. That nature is a dia-
lectical fire. That nature is

*   *   *

Long-suffering.

*   *   *

These moths, white, float in and out of Douglas fir, tribal
simples, grazing.

*   *   *

"The pleasure of the text." I treat myself to lunch at the
pub, sip cool gazpacho, snatch at "a poem about terror,"
leave when the noise level gets too high.

*   *   *

The pools of the damned reflect a bloodstained eye, it stares, bull's eye, I say, on target, as usual.

*   *   *

A dartboard at the pub jabbed and jabbed again. Rules of the game. Class, analysis. The old Dad's Cookies factory where I first read Marx: friable proportions – or that's the way the cookie crumbles. Dearie.

*   *   *

I practise tangential existence – necessity, economy, art, use. Big words, small world, bombarded by particle physicists – and butterflies whose effects are infinite.

*   *   *

Musical interlude. Tralalala-la. I pack my things. Largo doloroso. Adagio for strings. I strangle a scream in the wrong key. The little fish jump up, nevertheless, scales shining. Stravinsky's firebird sings in the heavenly shade-tree, *con fuoco*.

Scattered Effects

"AMBROSIA"

Bee-sweet, the honey now / how trails a star
of far / near hawthorn and roseate late leap year

Gerard Manley, your black cassock
rushing through cosmic and microcosmic

inscaped latitudes. I look, see you
passing away / through Jesuitical

raced time-future. All your musculature
stretched, taut, reaching out / off

from black clouds, momentary passage,
there to here, tears of *your* Christ

mix / mingle "I am so happy, so happy,"
your last wet watering words,

June the 8th's hawthorn-hoped, pied beauties,
beatitudes, 1889, heard

here, February, leapings of '88,
10:15 a.m. The 24th.

"EVENSONG"
(even song syllabics)

Tending toward music, the artist's
life tends toward solitary notes, slips
of the tongue, hand, eye, eerily like
intelligence of higher orders.
Hierarchical systems of dream
stuff, choirs of angelic lisps, minty
panpipes accompanying dawn, mist
rising from hills, green splits, gold flecks, flicks
of day ascending. No one goes home.
They're out and about, lured by goat god
music-food into noon sun hot rays,
bothered, skewered on oily spit, fat
and famished; one note more, another
tugs them into laid-back afternoon,
lawlessness. Wine, sun sets their steps on
cool path's mythic return, labouring
all the way home. Quiet entrances,
doffed hats, feet on wood, stone, a chair, and
evensong's slim, uncanny sibilance.

"ANAXIMANDER"
610–546? BC

for Smaro Kamboureli

Nectar, attar of roses, gardenias gaze from the shade.
Anaximander sits on a rock inventing the patient sun-
dial. He sits on a rock in the Greek style, bathed in
primary matter, puzzled, at home in his puzzlement,
the grand motions of the universe, his minutes slipping
away.

*   *   *

For me, too, it was garden, that day the rufous humming-
bird bounced in the spray of the hose as I watered the
roses. Inspired – roses, hummingbird, and me – precisely
because of the boredom of how things are, and nectar.

*   *   *

The Grand Unified Theory. A crystal ballroom lined with
mirrors. Reflection. To be whole, seen from all sides at
once, make sense.

*   *   *

Gold watch on my wrist, gold sun on the land, move-
ment and shadows. Milesian godfather, cartographer as
well as why not everything?

*   *   *

Yes. No. Two words are better than one during the para-
digm shift. Spit and hold your finger to the wind. Which
way is blowing? Is blowing the lid off your head? Is prose.
Poem?

*   *   *

Dr. Melzack applies electrodes to the lab cat's brain. I
want to die. I want to die again. The good doctor, they
say, they say, for your own good.

*   *   *

I sit on a rock in the wood and study the mosses. The bosses of philosophy pace up and down, auras of fanatic gold pulsing around them.

*   *   *

I tap my own temple. It taps back an undeciphered code, an ode to spring, perhaps, to the skylark, nightingale, pleased with its own whistling.

*   *   *

Rose-coloured glasses, a shift in the mood, or indigo, odd angles, surfaces like mica, cosmos and microcosmos, glazed and changing.

*   *   *

His One substance. Opposing powers. Those silly wheels of fire, the planets orbiting.

"ATTEND"
for Sharon Thesen

Between "attached" and "aloft"
getting the poem on the page
a voice tells her on this day
attend.
Harrowed she is, anguished
by this day's dailiness
teenaged son in danger
following forwardness
as the poem records Bach
in invisible margins, neighbour
pruning his shrubs, her baby-
sitter sorting out her own love-
life at Bino's Pancake House.

This is the way the world –
this is the way I pick up on
the voice in my head today
offering Valium, substance
long gone, used up in my last
big job and love affair,
its breakdown. *Velvet*, it leads
me on, vole, variorum, text to –
– *stumbling block*, unblocked
and falling over myself in files,
folios, fricatives, freesias – ah
freesias, the scent, spring, sickness,
planting now in Fall my hyacinths –
you brought me hyacinths – and Edith
Sitwellian rain, bombs falling
on London, that old poverty.

So I go, so she
sits at her desk, attending.
To wedding plans, Matisse in the
offing, possible poems
feared and held off for a moment
in her new life, or old one
revised, rough-drafted in the
coil of my cigarette smoke, my next
word being "lavender." Lavender
Allen, childhood friend, far back,
Victorian Lavender's innocence
gone surely by now, my own
purple's vengeance, as Bach
counterpoints his clear-eyed
fingering of her poems and mine,
the free play, the scandal
murmuring in shrubs this strange
infinitive (listen, I can't believe
it) – *to frolic.*

An editor asks me to put it all down: the reasons I write. And I thought "it" was a gift. *Homo ludens* at play among the killing fields of dry grasses. Playful woman making a space to breathe. "There *are* the poems," Sharon says, she means, between the critical flash. There *are* the poems, like fists wearing birthstones and bracelets, her "roses & bliss." Or they're like legs running, bounding over the fields of force, momentum, for a quick roll in Darwin's tangled bank. And there are the poets doing what? And why, the editor asks. What does he want? Contributions to knowledge? Civilization and its discontents? Chaos among the order – or, oh yes, French doors opening onto a deck and a small pool where we can watch our weird reflections shimmering and insubstantial? The proper response to a poem is another poem. We burrow into the paper to court in secret the life of plants, the shifty moon's spacewalks, the bliss, the roses, the glamorous national debt. Someone to talk to, for God's sake, something to love that will never hit back.

"PEPPER TREE"

The pepper tree opens its arms
to the fifth of March
it greets the fog
and rabbits springing
across a heath
somewhere in Scotland.
It believes in Henry Miller
and that other bastard Picasso.
It believes in its own genius,
suddenly, after winter.
It shines with land claims.
It turns with the hidden sun
praising Winnie Mandela
and Nelson
and Cory Aquino
it roots itself
down into this small-minded pot of darkness
and – *illico* – spins out into
the whirlwind.
It finds ecstatic form by changing places.
It changes places.

MESSAGES

They are always projecting themselves.
Cats play to cats we cannot see.
This is confidential.
—Letter from E.D. Blodgett

The young psychic comes back from halfway down the hall
to tell me to write about the cat on the postcard
tacked to the wall above my typewriter.
There is an understanding between us, and I show her
a photo in the *Journal* where the cat appears behind
my shoulder –

A piece of politics. A creature of state.

Out of Ptolemy's reign, cast in bronze (earrings restored)
far from Egypt now in its northern home.
Probable use: to hold the bones of a kitten.
Representative on this earth of the goddess Bastet.

She prances toward me down the ramp of the poem
sent to me by the young psychic who is writing
an historical novel.
She moves toward me through an aura composed
of new light and the golden dust of Ptolemy.
Halfway down the ramp her high ears turn against
the task of the poem toward allurements
of stockmarket and monopoly.

Cats play to cats we cannot see.

Now it is night, I have locked her in this pyramid
of my own free will. She toys with the unwinding
sheet of a mummified king, paws at royal jewels
and sighs.
As I sleep at the 5 a.m. poem's edge she sniffs my skin
for news of her old lost world.

She names the princes as they pass
heading for Bay Street in the winter blight.

They are always projecting themselves.
This is confidential.

Now it is morning in North Nineteen Hundred and Eighty.
The message clear: price of gold slumps,
war cracks at the border.
The Queen's cold mouth sends warning:

Beware.

How to get out of the poem without a scratch?
Each cast of the line seductive and minimal.
The ramp of the poem folding against
the power of the cat.
Possible use: to hold the bones of little ones
who cannot speak for themselves
or the goddess Bastet.

Possible worth: treasure beyond speech
out of the old tomb, out of the mind's
sarcophagus. Wanting to touch
wanting to stare at her agate eyes
in the dark night of a museum postcard.

Bastet!
She moves toward me. She is here –
HISS HISS
With one paw raised
she scratches the final hieroglyphs
at the end of a bronze poem
I cannot see.

Gwen, I didn't know it had been so bad, such a long way down these past months to the *Afterworlds*, or that the door and the blue wings opened and closed in that sound of death you said you knew the tune of. Your last poems so big with cosmos & semen & gold – and I'm afraid adjectives that came too easily over the years: *terrible, beautiful, splendid, fabulous, wonderful, remarkable, dark, exquisite, mighty* – all of which you were as your cat waited to take over the typewriter and get on with its sublime works while you were out colliding with Barker Fairley in a metaphysical blizzard or handing a coin to the ferryman for the last ride.

The Loneliness of the Long Distance Poet. Red Curtains. The White Horse. Late Song. A Stillness of Waiting. The Death of the Loch Ness Monster in the vast spaces of the subatomic world where Matter has a   tendency to exist ... Here where events have a   tendency   to occur ...

As you lay there dying in seizure was it your lord Life or your lord Death who came to collect a last poem as you careened into *the beautiful darkness*? And was it really beautiful? Tell me. Was it dark? Or did the cat get your last fabulous word?

CUE CARDS

Fabulous fold of the grey cloud
over the banked white one –

Stolen thunder. Stolen gold.

Heart of the jungle darkness.
Hot death. Rousseau and Conrad

meet at the riverbank
stare at their outstretched hands

that hold no clues.
Clueless. Monsieur Rousseau

falls down in a faint
seeing stars and shepherdesses.

And Mr. Conrad stumbles on
lured by drumbeats.

Half dead at the end of
his story, he leaves his trail –

and another Rousseau, Henri,
paints stripes on a large cat

as it royally passes through customs.

"DIPLOMATIC POUCH"

Alfred Hitchcock steers his stomach across
the screen, a pregnant pause in the action,
the pit of wit. A note passes from hand
to hand, a message on form and function;
female fear splits the bathroom tiles,
"improved binoculars," "Pain fountain."
The romantic couple cast long glances
and smoke from their silver lair; birds
zoom down like missiles, testing, testing?

I loved the sophistication of every move,
sly camera angles, clues and accents, that
touch of class. And the neurotic gloss
on the whole murderous enterprise, the old
master's nasty mind that took us for
what we were worth.

"THINKING CAP"

The red hat
sails
through a rift
in my skull
out and over the
waiting audience
it's the colour of
red peppers
it's a flying
saucer
hovering there
spying and spritely
elvish in the coy
mood of not being
a red wheel
barrow
as mute though
as silent-speaking
this thing / spinning
over your head
preparing to land
fasten your seatbelt
lady and don't smoke
we're coming in
to Williamsland
to invade
the objects
to snatch the
afterimage of
ol' Bill's plums –
you know –
the ones that
tasted so good
because they were
cold and beautiful
and couldn't

speak

"CAT & MOUSE GAME"

The cat steps over
   the rules of the game
     he, she, it crosses

the green playing field
   this is where I lie down
     to smell the daisies.

Mouse comes out of her house
   doing everything wrong
     thinks I'm a sunny day

which I think so too
   sprawled here pondering
     law and order.

J'accuse, j'accuse,
   j'accuse!
     Have I struck

the right note?
   I exit the scene
     paring my fingernails.

The field surges behind me
   with fun & names
     disrupting the bloody text.

PERFORMANCE

Who is this *I* infesting my poems? Is it I hiding behind the Arno type on the page of the book you are reading? Is it a photograph of me on the cover of *Wilson's Bowl*? Is it I? *I* said, *I* say, *I* am saying –

I am the mask, the voice, the one who begins those lyrical poems, *I wandered lonely as a cloud ... I hear the Shadowy Horses, their long manes a-shake ... I am of Ireland / And the Holy Land of Ireland ... I, the poet William Yeats ... I am worn out with dreams ...*

Or am I reading, as they say, "in person," in the first person? I step up to the microphone. I wait for you to cough with my damaged lungs. "*I* am with you." The poem ends. I move into my higher consciousness, my lower voice, my sense of the present, my invocation, my prayer, my tiny faith in the typewritten words before me. The poem begins.

Listen: Do you hear the *I* running away with the man in the green hat? Look again. *I* is off and diving into Fulford Harbour to run with the whales. *I* spout. *I* make whale song. Passengers on the ferry swarm to starboard to see me disporting myself. *I / we* know they are out to get us. Yes, they are mad for education. They'll pen us up at Sealand and we'll die. We don't build big and we can't shoot. *I* commits suicide in the watery commune, the vocal pod. *We* swims on.

I am performing this poem thinking of bill bissett at whose last performance he did not perform. He put on a record and left the room – "wow," as bill would say. But the whales have made it through Active Pass. They pass on the message: *Put on the record.* Sonar pulses ring for miles. Paul Horn is in the Temple of Heaven playing flute ... *Put on the record.*

I devise. You devise. We devise. To be together briefly with the page, the fallen timber. Or with me here standing before you wondering if the mike is on, if my mask is on, *persona*, wondering what to read next, or whether you'll turn the page. Like the state, I do not wither away, though the end is near.

I enter The Edge of Night. I join the cast of General Hospital. *I hear the Shadowy Horses, their long manes a-shake* … I am only a partial fiction. Look. I hand you a golden jonquil. *Here. Now. Always.* On the outgoing breath of the whales.

The woman takes the ferry to Salt Spring Island, proceeds to the local Pharmasave, which is ablaze with irrelevance and consumer goods. It's where we all come to. Pharmaceuticals and sleaze, cat food, toilet paper, makeup, deodorants, sweatshirts, stationery, chocolate bars, soap, et cetera.

This is Paradise, the tourist brochures and I say so. Hundreds of acres of trees are being clear-cut today, here, right now, to produce the paper to advertise the sleaze, vitamin pills, corn removers, hair removers, cleansing creams, biscuits, jujubes, hair clips, fingernail polish, earrings, scissors, toothpaste, Timex watches.

She walks the long aisle and aims for the pharmacist. She demands 100 Seconal and 100 dollars, and says she has a gun, which she hasn't. The pharmacist counts out 100 pills and five twenties. She ups the ante – another hundred. He counts again and when her hands are full he grabs her, and the RCMP arrive. It's Saturday.

Spring is already here in Ganges, in Paradise. Easter cards, chocolate bunnies, spring-coloured eggs, yellow ribbon for wrapping gifts. The resurrection. Condoms, jellies, foams, pills, magazines selling sex and beautiful B.C.

The woman from the Mainland, of no fixed address, is removed to Victoria, a little bit of Olde England. And then it's Monday. She's 39 and she's suicidal. They'll keep her in jail until a doctor comes – perhaps on Wednesday.

This story is taking far too long to tell, but this is an exceptional event for the local Pharmasave. What a Saturday, they say, as it turns into legend, and right after *that* another woman comes in and we catch her shoplifting! But what did she lift: toothbrush, Tampax, iron pills, flea collar, vaginal spray, videotapes, alarm clock, perfume, shampoo, peroxide, garbage bags?

The mythological proportions of the story are splendid, if obvious. Eve, the first woman to be seduced by advertising and deathwish, is at it again, agog with superabundance and enclosure, slightly west, south and light years east of Eden.

BRONWEN'S EARRINGS

Long, or large and circular
the only decoration on her
tall frame, her plain facade
the better to hear the high
vibrations of your health, your
sorrows. A touch of fantastic
as she moved her head
to follow the plot
silver or gold flashing
hilarious light on the lure
of the pierced ear.
Spangles. Trapezoids, fluttery
things. Wild bird.

The pair I gave her
turquoise, oval, Chinese
I think and very long
with a history of survival.

As I drink this tea
on an ordinary day
someone crosses
a street in Kingston
picking up flute notes
soprano complaints
her earlobes tugged
by a small weight
of chimes
the need to be heard, desire.

THE MAKING OF A JAPANESE PRINT

The first plate in the volume is the key block giving the outline. It is easy to see how each successive color is added by a separate block to achieve the final result.
—*The Making of a Japanese Print*

Imprint No. 1

Eye contact, and it's forever.
The first circle.

And then the breast
the left or right.
So choice.
Or grab what is given.

Rosebud and at the
periphery / eyelash
dark sandals pass by.

Add a chair in the corner
with a white chemise.
This is the only way to go
– outward.

Door behind the mother
closing as father in blue
blows out.

White filled in, hatch-
crossings for negative space.
Decadent life.

Flesh tint laid on
with extreme caution.
All moves are dangerous:

open the door and wind pours in
with dust. Lift the head
of mother an inch
her attention goes
out the unseen window.

If baby sleeps
hand falling away from
the opening bud, rose
becomes dream, memory
a praise of distance.

*Technique is all
a test of the artist's
sincerity.* Oh
we are *sincere*, we go
for the blade, cut close
to the bone. The splotch
of red in the lower right-hand
corner, a sign of the happy
maker.

Imprint No. 2

Knife. Chisel. Mallet.
Block of cherry wood.
Printing pad. Paper. Ink.

What does he think?

He floats a green
into the space
of its assignation.
A world divides,
the view from an empty
chair shifts

a chair with a life of its own
an orange cushion.
Poppies arise from extinction
on the plane of the sun.

Harunobu, your hand trembles.
You will die young and lucky.
Sit down in the chair you
yourself have provided.
The curved form is a fan
alarmingly pink.
Flutter the air.

Intaglio for what you see best
the "empty imprint"?
What you see best
is the ivory kimono
coming towards you.
It will stay in the same place
always, Harunobu, brocading
the threat of advance.

A mere press of your hands
and your death flies
into a silken shadow.

Then washy blue three-quarters up.

Imprint No. 3

A fake. There was no chair
no washy blue in the "Heron Maid."
I made it up for my own artistic
purposes. I was thinking of
Van Gogh, of myself sitting down
for the last time and getting
up again to make this confession.

Tree, shrubs, a turquoise stream
a Japanese woman dressed for cold
her parasol a shield against the
snow which we can't see falling.
One ear pokes out, too high up
from under her brown hood
yet all is harmonious.

In the floating world
she stands quite still
like the snowy heron
who is really always moving.
She is also winter and tells me
more about herself than Harunobu
wanted me to know.

Imprint No. 4

The Heron Maid steps
on her wooden blocks
off the path
into summer.
She removes her winter
cloak, her sandals
dips her feet
in the turquoise stream.
What does she think
as she sits on the verge
this side of anonymous water?
She uncoils her hair
slips off her rings
imagines a different future.
She thinks of Harunobu
working away at his
butcher blocks
his famous seasons.

She'll have to change
habits and colours
wash off her fear,
Perhaps she'll look
for another job
cut her hair short
change her expression.
And, it's possible, die
some day in foreign arms
under the new dispensation.

Each block is laid on
with extreme caution
then set aside
out of harm's way.

A woman emerges at last
on the finest paper, cursing
his quest for the line
and this damned delicate fan
carved in her hand
to keep her forever cool
factitious, apparently pleasing.

Uncollected
and
Unpublished Poems

INVOLUTION

Sisyphus heaved hardening the rock in Hades
suffering great worlds of weight till now unknown
to fall back on him time and time again
the rock strutting to his chest
storing sharp with granite his stone's sin.

Rock became eye all-seeing knowing
the King come to this death-dealing
through his own gaining.
The eye took it to and fro from the hill's motion
and weeping, "Corinth! Corinth!" rolled in the vision
of Sisyphus chained to his own eye's prison.

Rock became planet revolved to mother
the King come to false labouring
through his unloving.
The planet wheeled to the axis of the hill's propulsion
and having Sisyphus the Tyrant devotion was doubled
to Corinth revenged by this involution.

Sisyphus thrusts hard the clock of time in Hades
suffering the great
fall proliferating ad infinitum
the sin and the fall and the effort upward;
the progress of no pilgrim
gaoled to a goal of stone.

NEW SNOW

If one were to walk carefully through snow
that is to say
      new snow

if one were to walk carefully
brothers would appear
          left and right

father would be in the centre
or trying to break the centre

          through

          new

             snow
this repetition of seasons and ages
would make no fine or delicate patterns

rather, snow
      being

       a wet

        dust

would more naturally nudge into crevices
or seep eventually into the earth
associating itself with old things

because it is new   simply because it is new

        or is it because in snow
there are family trees
          meriting stories

bearing truth with the earnest purity

        of bright reproduction?

STORIES

A mask discerned before
      is setting
         on a face
pleating the identities
            tidily into place.

A thought pursued before
      is trotting
         on the track
chipping the ancient earth
            steadily into flack.

An act rehearsed before
      is playing
         to an end
proving the locks of keys
            finally must command.

This pain walks old before
      its creeping –
         stamps a brand
tramping the definite body
            audibly into sound.

Rabbits intimidate her eyes
with their circular procreation
they clock with fertility
her eye's decay.

And I, in love with barrenness,
in hate fly from this
diseased increase.

And the rabbits wheel more numerous.

O God! I know there's only
my heart to give
to stop them dead with love
and drop rabbits unlimited
into the violet earth

and the beautiful earth
would coffin in beauty
this filthy crop of love.

BIRDS

Birds are shaken pepper in the sky

        spice in the eye

and highest fall

        where the dizzy die

folding the wind

        into their call

aspect, association, method in all

manoeuvering.

NECESSITY: ECONOMIC AND OTHERWISE

The quick flicked close to the dead
last night
and I, in righteous fear, lowered my head
to flight's
sleek pursuit of corners
to hide around –
discovered a territory foreign
yet bound, contiguous as a nation
bordering on compassion
for neighboured dead
but pressed by necessity to pick
the flesh and metal marrow of the quick.

WEATHER FORECAST

and it's half past snow time
no time for wastrel minutes
to delude us
intruding feet steep into
white pliancy
inaccurate as prophets
we embolden a plain blanket
with predictions:
say winter stoops to the virile
vowels of February
to venture a guess that March
the miracle sun, will blow in
yellows   and   the primitive green of June.

MESSIANIC

Hail me all holy
tell me like a lover
I am divine
a star, and hover
between your first
and last tomorrow
like a sign.

Tell me that this sign
suspends a lantern
to your mind
and lights up there
the sharpened wine.
Tell me I define
your sorrow
much as Christ
proffering hunger
for the morrow.
Teller of thrillers
hail me with lies
like a lover cry
that I toll the bell
behind the drastic day
and the signal night.

Tell me, tell me – oh spell
out that I am bright: a sign
a staff, a rod:
bright, a saviour,
flavour of God
savouring of Hell.

DUST INTO DUST

It is all given,
it is all given,
no more the hard slice of the melon moon
white to be taken.

It is all given at the fountains of the fish.
Grief and the wish are known for long,
but brief are the bones of fish.

No more the hand offers.
The hand is taken.
Hunger leads the hungry.
The starved are withheld.

The word is not written on the wall.
But the back is against it.
The body is given,
gone back into brick.
The act of the sensual fact is given.

And the clay does not resist.

LITTLE LINES

I turn my hand
into a soft fist
turning away wrath
holding my own anger
softly like a moth
in the curved palm.
Now the moth can read
my palm's lines:
this is my life
I tell the moth
this is the story
I've indented my flesh with.
Read if you can those
crooked paths
flicker your antennae
tickle my fancy
my hard heart
and all those little
lines I cannot read.
Decipher them if you can
as I hard the fist   this fist
for the blow.

QUICK RELIEF

Dr. Doubleday assures us the hypodermic
aids the more distressed gland to secrete
in a more normal fashion,
and the muse from the O.R. knows a miracle
mould flowers like a peace from wounds.

For we can be all easy, easy
We can be all easy.

Though rain still will fall with sound
it will write no metaphors for tears
(displayed in aesthetic tombs
they glisten as diamonds of the ancient sane,
sad in a sad museum).

For we will be all easy, easy
We will be all easy.

FERAL

the animals
curl up
on the red
square carpet
and sleep the sleep
of the just
or just sleep

the best of it is
that animals
manage to pass the dark away
on colour
then start at grey dawn's bite
to no style of guilt or fright
nor sickness at the built
scheme of analysis
of the quick
prehensile
night

NEW YEAR MESSAGE FOR J. ALFRED PRUFROCK

The road is long for us, Mr. Pru-
frock, in 1952.
                    Figuring yourself all
smartened up, unshocked since oh so
long ago unfrocked of all mysteries,
merriment, and imaginary mermaids –
to soothe you I will comb your hair
and part what is cleft to care –
and would it be, perhaps, unkind
if one should find your bright
politics now quartered in the socio-
sexual structure of the corner bank?
But they are there, I fear, and you
now take tea aware with lemon
and run to shun the measurements
of coffee. Oh yes, oh yes,
J. Alfred P., I can sense, indeed
foresee that here in this year
of yellowing words you will walk
strict with conservative love
telling birds not to bother you
and the stars to settle their own affairs.

"INTUITION OF A LITERARY WEEKEND"
for A.E.

Look alive!
           The joint is jumping
                 with cultivated fancies
strive to be picturesque, dearie
arrest detestable silences
contrive smart somersaults
              see, the intellect
              lands, bounces
stands with arms wide,
            announces
                  (a clown with a big mouth)
"The Greek boys and girls are coming out to hoot
and Look! They're putting on their gayway theatre boots!"
So toot your own horn dearie
the weary River Cataraqui
can't be fenced unless we form a claque,
we form a claque, a clique, a brick-a-brackerie
and all go down with Moses
                All Go Down!

A ROOM OF ONE'S OWN

Lying alone on the bed
and dreaming in the drift
of heavy poems –
Dante, Homer, ambivalent Joyce –
I lie in a comfortable close:
my lazy hair sprawls over the bowges
of Hell
and hands touch Ulysses entering
the City;
my own arrogant poems flaunt
on dictionaries and newspapers
and black slippers bow to each
other like gnats in a minuet;
while outside the dance of taxis
disturbs letters and essays
and the ambulance runs on its own
red stories in the street

             Oh all right!   Living
alone may not be tidy
but right now I'm full as a bee
that has buzzed all day into
many heads
then plumps on sultry pillows
to devour the messages
of modern and ancient flowers.

IDIOT BIRDS

The idiot birds
strut the lawn.
Summer gives them all
they've ever wanted.
They cheep, they chime,
they scratch the dawn.
Idiot birds! Summer is all
they've wanted.

But then the fools
in ignorant bliss
ascend in the singing air
as we like noisy idiots strut
in our summer of despair.

CROSSWORDS

He it is I most admire
　　but his past I can't acquire
therefore decline to copy him.

She it is I most desire
　　but her future would expire
socially, were I to press this whim.

Me it is they both would like
　　to drown in bleak pools of night
but crossword purposes of love
　　prove puzzles' vertical will thread
horizons with mirages to remove

till words, warped into squares of right
　　will, of themselves, fall dead.

SONNET

The child turned and left the house
and then the house turned on me
and all the elements of love
cried for the constancy of us.

In grasses of the labouring night
illumination caught the blade,
then in the first unfinished birth
I cried and broke with infant light.

Though children fall on bitter grass
and houses weep for what was said,
I turn, return the wounded earth
and move the stone which would not bless.

Hearts hallow now the life in death.
We are the children of the love we made.

ISHMAEL

There is so much sea,
a permanent crisis of loneliness,
an intimate eternity, and God, and the white, infinite
Mother,
and I am but a name.
Call me Ishmael,
for the sky beyond portends potential sea
and fear is around me
and death by water sure
as grass is green,
certain as the pitiful grain
of sand contrives a desert
to pretend a land.
I am the name
adrift upon a broken coffin raft.
I pray, in hungry solitude decay.
The sea is lonely.
Call me Ishmael.
May my day be done,
and the gull of whiteness sing.

ASTRONAUT

"I am well, I am cheerful." His message zooms
to Khrushchev and to God.
I too catch his unearthly voice in print.
And I am pleased with Yuri Gagarin.
And I am well, I am cheerful.
The infinite at last exposed.

ALEX

at five o'clock today Alex four years old said
I will draw a picture of you!
at first he gave me no ears and I said
you should give me ears
I would like big ears one on each side
and he added them and three buttons down the front
now I'll make your skirt wide he said and he did
and he put pins in all up and down my ribs and I waited
and he said now I'll put a knife in you
it was in my side and I said does it hurt
and No! he said and we laughed and he said
now I'll put a fire on you and he put male
fire on me in the right place then scribbled me
all into flames shouting FIRE FIRE FIRE
FIRE FIRE FIRE and I said
shall we call the fire engines and he said Yes!
this is where they are and the ladders are bending
and we made siren noises as he drew the engines on
over the page then he said the Hose! and he put
the fire out and that's better I said
and he rolled over laughing like crazy
because it was all on paper

POEM

A ship named *Dimitrios*
                    sits in the river
                                        rusting
the river is quiet
                    unperturbed
by the rust
or the fishermen's strike
the fishermen are still
                                fishing

it is after six
                    the sun incurious
and hot

my double loves touch me
                                very simply

all this is normal

but Duncan's book
                    in my lap
the quietness of the river
                                in my eyes
and Robert reading
                    a memory of mastery
                                        which hurts.

pearl poem
white with virtue
or opal
marred, shining
hold out for the moment
when you'll be heard
then speak
from the absolute
location
of your mist

FOR ROBERT DUNCAN

"In myself I am desolate"
but the other self, "the poet self"
threads a melodic theme out of griefs
and snows, goes to wisdom and gladness.
We listened intently. We were a room.
We were a silence waiting for the high
absolute note of a fixed star to enter
our ears. It entered. We went forward
together in that sadness that wills us.

In myself I know we were together
knew we were going.

In the narrow chamber separating the self
from the self we listen alone to a bell
echoing in virtue, applauding itself
in absolute time. By virtue
of this bell the selves keep distant
respect each for the other, know
their longing for music.

CONTINUUM

Nothing can be undone, least of all
the darkness of history and the fact
of one's birth.
Those are the major premises that come
to us to be gathered.

I have walked into the sea intending
to go the limit and found myself asking
Napoleon to – for God's sake   stop playing
Marlon Brando.
I have taken the measure of my breath
because that is a law of poetry
and measured my life under the law
of pride.

So much for the personal statement.

History is too big to talk about,
though I will say it oscillates, is not
an abstraction, not the retention of facts.
It's a feeling, the way a day opens.
Or maybe it's more like a poltergeist
that knocks over hat stands and snatches
a pipe out of the mouth of a burnt-out professor.

We are never abandoned.

Nothing can ever be undone or rejected.
Today I wired the prime minister, who
is not Napoleon, STRONGLY URGE CANADA
DISSOCIATE ITSELF FROM AMERICAN POLICY
IN VIETNAM

and wept because my grief seemed to be my own.

Multiple me's and you's in the "Mirrored
Room" in Fubbalo's Albright-Knox. Table without
top, chair without a bottom. Don't sit! You could
land nowhere somewhere in Alice-glass floor or
ceiling. A case of light with no safety for dreams
at the depths of self or sea. Head and feet
meeting infinitely and diminishing. Not multi-
foliate rose vision of white but transmigration
of image inverted / upright. Music and mathematics
cage of glass where freedom is in these entrances
informed on exactly how we stand now.

The denial of one's neighbour is
easy / as
denial of one's self / the me
-keeping silence.
But to hold the alert passions
pointing around the sun is
what must be done
beloved (oh my!) America / lost
land of the New Found
-ling conscience. Do the sun
flowers over the border still
find their heads to the sun?
What Is To Be Done? The old
sob of Chernyshevsky who /
holding his head to the wall of the
great cell of Russia / how many
years ago / cried out some
kind of answer. But now "to be
done" is what harrows us / here
in our Iceland / here in our me-
keeping silence of no letters no
poems policy right action ever /
and ever the empty prevarications of
"I am sorry for the delay." Who wants
you for a neighbour? You hit
at the hope of whoever believed
Vanzetti and Sacco ("Those
beautiful clove flowers surprised me so deeply
in my unrest heart …") once lay / in
the palm of your justice. They learned
the hard way. Died with the grace
of the pure in heart.
But how shall we die who are not /
pure not pure?

And if the burning bush is not the
Spirit in-living who's to say
that the saffron robe dancing in flames
is the phoenix arising?

There are too many heroes these days
and a sweet nostalgia for wisdom.
I would not judge in a book of /
judgment. I can kill with a word or
the keeping-me-silence / or
turn my sunflower head to that
Burn Baby Burn!
/ or the now-coming-love of
perhaps or at least a short season
/ or Shanti shanti shanti
as an / old cat said
(Mistah Kurtz – he dead?)
and sunflower seeds are
for parrots?

NOTES FROM AN UNUTTERED REVOLUTION

I.

Even impossibilities
arrive like
crowns on velvet
cushions. Crowned
we are heads of
state, elegant
and able. We nod
subversion
to each other
across our
kingdom.
Mozartian flutes
accomplish
jewelled
embellishments.

II.

Macbeth and his lovely lady
the blood between them
is that the image
the brutal bond
shrewd music
of the sombre forms;
plumed death's head
blossoming among
the hair
the roses.

III.

These possibilities these
off-spring spring off
into their terrorism
tumble upon playground
and open spaces
take aim from ground level
amid rubble
mount guns on bastions of finance
snipe from dead towers
let dream castles fall
from the air
fall
into dwelling.

RICHARD II

"Synoptic
                    spectacles
         the better to see
                    the pageantry of
     'multiform antithetical influx'
I smell
        you smell
                    we all smell
         carnal plants
                    effulgent in darkness
                    INCARCERATION
        let my mind reach ...
kind thoughts   kind deeds
                         every day in
      every – I grow
                 better   and
         What time is it!
                        Has that watch
on your wrist accompanied all this shit?
                     your imperial schizophrene
        goosed   gangbusted   shaven
                              every day
      in every
               What is it!   Nothing
  Please pay the bill
  I can't pay the bill
                The men you ...
  Ah let down your
                 guard
                    you know you
         can always trust me
      Here is my kingdom here is my crown
            'And here is not a creature but myself'
  still breeding
            thoughts
  Are those screams birthpangs milady
            poor little baby
                    poor little man"

ANTISONG

Bitterness rolls off
my tongue
ancestors roll off
my tongue
family living and present
wet my taste buds
spittle of little
pasts
viscous attachments and
venom
words heave off my tongue
heraldic caskets

    dog   eyes
        return   Orphic
            vomit   profundo

        "'It's a poor memory that only works
        backwards,' the Queen remarked."

"THE KING OF KINGS HAS LEFT THE PEACOCK THRONE"

CBC Radio News, January 16, 1979

The King of Kings has left the Peacock Throne,
a languorous, long, courtly getaway.
The Shah will make the Yankee sun his own.

You heard the quake kick up God's sticks and stones?
A January omen, would you say?
The King of Kings has left the Peacock Throne.

The cars are honking in the streets of bone.
The people dance and kiss a different way.
The Shah will make the Yankee sun his own.

The ones who died street fighting would have known
that Allah chose Iran and not L.A.
The King of Kings has left the Peacock Throne.

Oh Persian oil and flesh and foreign loans,
Oh jewelled and Swiss accounted disarray.
The Shah will make the Yankee sun his own.

And now Khomeini comes to say he's won,
But where is Roloff Beny and his camera – eh?
The King of Kings has left the Peacock Throne.
The Shah will make the Yankee sun his own.

FOR MICHAEL

You send a peacock card – bird
with a fat blue (blue!) stomach
of feathers. Ridiculous, Michael,
you come from a far country and bird
comes too flapping its wings to land here
on this desk, its crying tail spread, and
I hear a mystic scream, an easy grieving.
But, Michael, it dances now, here on small
feet, insisting you write like a crazed
Canadian, running the family through,
touching occasionally your feather-blue
eyes lightly, shading them.

It was just there. It? They? Music
suddenly I come upon the
                           key cutting shop
and "Wool" and a young bassist – bronzed hair long
beyond her waist
                 Music
in the courtyard of the Centre. One can smoke
and listen to Music with little kids
lying on stomachs
                         escalator climbing with surprised
mid-day Edmontonians playing it cool
         who look askance
                         or turn around as the
Music mounts with them into leafy levels
of Marks and Spencer's
                       staring –
The Edmonton Symphony in plain clothes fiddling
the bad vibes of Eaton's and Woodward's, key shop
grinding out keys.
                  Keys!
And after the final number I'm sure I see
Maureen Forrester licking a vanilla ice cream cone …
– she waves her musical hand to a friend in the winds.
Man in cowboy hat wanders off. Chinese gentleman
moves urgently towards Exit. Maureen takes
the escalator, strolls into Mappins.
Touchstone. She is touchstone. Remember Maureen
the Trout Quintet that summmer of '51 in Montreal?
But maybe it isn't Forrester, after all. Thirty
years later, almost, I am here
carrying nonbiodegradable plastic shopping bags
back
       to the scary carpark
                            jangling my keys.

SITTING, 1982

I am sitting in the basement bedroom of the Schubarts' house. I am sitting on the floor and the floor is covered with pears. Yes, pears. I have come down here for a few minutes of meditation before the benefit concert begins. Maggie said the room was full of pears and the room is full of pears. They are lolling around in the most astonishing self-absorption: that is, they would be if they had selves to absorb. Obviously these are Zen pears who could turn into wine, but of course they won't do that by just lying around down here, no more than I could. No. They are here, like me, for a small rest, waiting to turn from green to gold or from gold to darker gold, with maybe a few brown spots.

Either these are Zen pears or they are Cézanne pears and when Eleanor comes down to use the bathroom, which is right next door to this room, she looks in at me and says, What are you doing down here? And then she sees the pears and says, Oh, the pears! Yes, aren't they wonderful, I say, and then

Don Erikson comes in and he says, What are you doing down here? And then he sees the pears and says, Oh, the pears! And it's as if they have just been shaken from the tree. I'm trying to collect myself, I say, as Hank peers over Don's shoulder, and they go away. The pears have rolled into a sort of trapezoid pattern and their fleshiness is humbling in this night without a moon. Or if there is a moon there isn't enough of one to shine in here and light up these plump pears.

There's no light in this room but there is a light in the hall and so the light that does get in touches only the tops of the pears. Upstairs the crowd is gathering and Paul and Susan and Oscar are tuning up their guitars and there is going to be this splendid concert in aid of Amnesty.

These pears have never heard of Amnesty International. But even better they have never heard of torture, mass executions, etc., etc. They are just lying here, lolling here, casually emitting the perfume of pure pear as I try to gather myself together. They don't want to be touched so I don't touch them. I sit and wait for them to move.

I guess I have to go upstairs now. Goodbye, pears, you happy family of one season and no parents, no grand-parents, no children, just you turning into the universe. I have already written one poem called "Two Pears: A Still Life" but that was a long time ago and tonight I have come upon a veritable throng of pears. Goodbye, goodbye, as I go upstairs.

Where everyone is looking happy at the big success we are about to have. We are all very pleased with ourselves and that we are so many. Even my doctor is here and she is nursing her little baby in a contented way. Susan is about to sing about becoming a mother and Oscar will sing about the Indians and the Hudson's Bay Co. Paul will play Villa-Lobos and a composition by a Cuban who was a political prisoner when he wrote his music. Way back when.

Everywhere the killings go on. Everywhere the new barba-rism. Andy is spreading out fabrics from a South African co-op. He is serious. I am nervous. Gary is nervous. Ann and Murray are not (they are studying Buddhism). Sheila arrives with wine. For a whole year now we have worked together and Meg's sprained ankle is finally mending. The dollars are pouring in like pears.

Now we must all sit down on the floor. I have also written a poem called "Sitting." Way back when, while everywhere the ...

This is a beautiful home made for music. Up on Mt. Tuam the Buddhists begin their prayers. In *communitas*. Paul strides in with his guitar. We sit now very quietly, as if we'd just been shaken from the tree ...

October 17, 1982

PRISON REPORT

The eye of Jacobo Timerman looks through the hole and sees
another eye looking through a hole.

These holes are cut into steel doors in prison cells in Argentina.

Both eyes are wary.
They disappear.

Timerman rests his cheek on the icy door,
amazed at the sense of space he feels – the joy.

He looks again: the other's eye is there,
then vanishes like a spider.

Comes back, goes, comes back.

This is a game of hide-and-seek.
This is intelligence with a sense of humour.
Timerman joins the game.

Sometimes two eyes meet at exactly the same moment.

This is music. This is love
playing in the middle of a dark night
in a prison in Argentina.

My name is Jacobo, one eye says.
Other eye says something, but Jacobo can't quite catch it.

Now a nose appears in the vision field
of Timerman. It rubs cold edges of the hole,
a love rub for Jacobo.

This is a kiss, he decides, a caress,
an emanation of solitude's tenderness.

In this prison everything is powered electrically
for efficiency and pain. But tenderness is also
a light and a shock.

An eye, a nose, a cheek resting against a steel door
in the middle of the dark night.
These are parts of bodies, parts of speech,
saying,
I am with you.

DON'T ASK ME

The light arising never has been darkness.
I would let you know if the red / dawn star
crenellated into systems. I would let you know
about the sun even the black sun if I could
tell you of "shapeless radiance."
Ask the yogi. Don't ask me. He points
to his guts' shine in the ablutions
of the holy morning.

FOLLOWING

for Daphne Marlatt

Botticelli – I say it
and the chord breaks
into its component parts
                                    la li   la li

That which is beautiful in Botticelli
disintegrates,
gathers again in women:
a woman in white,
a lily,
a dream in the eye
of Botticelli.

He is standing apart
from *Primavera*.
He is painting forever
her in this full moon
winter's night.

A woman in light
leans out and over me,
waving a wand
of old language
unspoken beyond
these words,
touching the black and white keys
of the walnut piano.

(Glenn's last session in the studio
also producing the pure, the immaculate
art of circumstances.)

Her white sails crossing the water –

I follow:
a flower is held out
and placed in the shell of Venus
who rises, wet,
to greet her.

HOW THE INDIANS GOT LEFT OUT OF THE BUSINESS OF PATRIATING THE CONSTITUTION

1. Although they are all members of first families, they
   do not sit at the same table as the Eatons and Southams.

2. Although they are the biggest landowners in the country,
   not one has the correct address.

3. Not one is the premier of an oil-rich province, or even
   an oil-poor province, and therefore cannot attend First
   Ministers' conferences and dinners and be interviewed
   by Patrick Watson on *The Watson Report*.

4. Although they know the uses of tobacco and the peace pipe,
   not one can handle a cigarette with the style of Lévesque.

5. They do not own corporations and their eyes do not glint
   with the brilliance of the Big Deal. They are not in
   Rotterdam one day, Johannesburg the next, and Calgary
   or Dallas a day later.

   They are here,
   dying and hiring lawyers.
   They are here.
   They meet the press.
   They hire more lawyers.
   They see how the legislatures of this country
   are stuffed with lawyers:

   criminal lawyers
   constitutional lawyers
   corporation lawyers
   civil and uncivil lawyers.

   They know the Law is an ass.
   They know that Justice must be seen to be done.
   They do not often see it.

   They are dying,
   but they are learning the power of contempt.

They are dying of mercury poisoning
yet they take up the tools of their art
and retrieve their beautiful languages, their signs.
They are dying in every prison in this country
and learning the System as fast as they can.

They dispatch their messengers to the Queen of England
and march on Ottawa, the city of tulips.
They do not mention the prime minister in their prayers.
They do not imitate him by wearing a rose in the lapel.
He does not enter even their worst dreams.

They are too busy –
dying and repatriating themselves
to their own country,
to the ruined land.

MEMO FROM HUBERT AQUIN, 1986

For the thin poets
who come out of the Blue
into this place of departure:
Je suis un peuple défait
qui marche en désordre
dans les rues qui passent
au-dessous de notre couche ...

The next episode introduces
the round fat body of the
intertextual critic
reading *Hamlet*
comme-çi, comme-ça
under blue Canadian skies.

Point: Papa Doc was seen entering
the Allan Memorial Institute
followed by *son fils et sa femme.*
They vanish through the back door.
Erasure.

Is it all a mistake?
This Seventh Heaven,
this Ninth Circle of Hell?
We are fat or thin,
gathered in the netherworld.
Here we go round again,
around and about in
the *Opel bleue* –
Vite, car je suis sur le point
de céder à la fatigue historique ...

Circulez. Circulez!

slag heaps, lost chords
the trombone mute of jazzman
humps his sounds and then that
low-down gutsy thrum of the doped-up
drummer bounces a steady mood down to
New Orleans.
Sad Blues or Le Jazz Hot, you gotta
get outta that place, man, ya gotta
bawl and wail, take to the cracked-up
Motown streets.

The Virgin drifts off in a blue canoe.
The river is running with salmon spawn, but
she doesn't notice.
She's dressed in a gown of grey chiffon, straw
hat crowned with flora. Pretty Puss. I knew
her once in a far countree.
Churr. Churr.
She's safe in the weathery distance now.
A cloud descends to pluck her heavenward, up,
up and away, she holds a big balloon, bombs
me with rosebuds, she's pedalling hard.

"CARAPACE"

The Emily Dickinson of the insect
world, but in red and black, I've
always loved her – *Ladybug*. She shines
and glistens, harmless-seeming –
Domestically – needling her way through
the extended metaphor, feeding herself
on Great Circumference, a leaf Design.

But see her now on my wrist, little
automobile, her carapace wards off
blows from the vengeful Puritan who
would hit – her – brittle Verse, its
glorious rust-stained Redness, its
wicked dots – of – Black.

THE DAY ARLENE HAD THE FLU

and overdosed on Aspirin and the doctor refused
to believe she wasn't even *aware* of overdosing,
didn't know how many she'd taken,
like too many poets coming to visit, staying too
long, she didn't *notice*.

(I am an Aspirin, said the poet, a real pill.
You can hardly taste me. Have another.)

The antidote: Jazz, and all that real life you
can't help noticing down in the dumps,

the *reverb* of one-uh, two-uh, three tickling her
ribs, sexy and brassy. She throws in some laughs
– and *laughs* – as it all adds up.

THE TREE SPEAKS

Get off my back,
I've had it up to here
with the humans,
let me grow old in peace,
fall over and die gracefully;
though I sometimes think
a quick cut of the chainsaw
is better than death by fire,
always a possibility.
Suffering. We know about
suffering. Growth is suffering.
But you know that.
And don't give me your stupid
human hugs. Listen to me now,
talking out of character like
a member of the human race,
look what you've brought me to,
so low that I'm only a foolish
projection of some old woman poet.

I have to listen to the ants,
beetles, lichen, chipmunks, mosses,
moulds, using my bark – and don't strip
it off me for your baskets, either.
Do you hear the raven up there
in my top-most boughs, tricking
and treating? I like that. I like
the feel of all that.

No, I don't want your hugs. I'm
sorry, or the chainsaw gangs,
or tongues of flame. Don't want
this poisoned voice. That old
woman can have it back.
I've got to save my breath.

Let me winter back into pure
tree life, species specific,
blowin' in the wind,
uttering only rarely a bleak
humanoid word
of thanks, of praise.

"REVISION"

I slice the flesh of an old poem
I started for you in 1957
called "Mangoes for Leonard Cohen"
the lines fall away
flesh that is often lost

Now I slice into the luminous
mangoes like a surgeon
the delight in my eyes
as they behold the broken tissue
is the delight of the skilful surgeon

My tongue on the golden flesh
is not just one instrument
remembering Eros but music as Eros
composing the perfect mango
as they move.

THE CAT GUARDING THE GATE

A Chinese godlet, tortoiseshell
hunched: *"Do Not Disturb*
me or the woman inside
the threshold of pain."

This he / she from the
heavenly cat kingdom
refuses to budge
for the Honda Accord.
"Take off, back up
with your good intentions
your careful word.
This is the gate of retrieval."

In bed, you Beth, Elizabeth,
with the rapist morphine,
dream's molester,
advance and retreat
with tides and myth
advance and retreat –
familial skin in the
process of Being
done in, peeled off, shed
for the mystic flesh
of the water snake
beached below your balcony,
Shamanic, summoning.

MAUREEN READING
for Stephen

She passes into a state of affairs
upheld by architecture and the sound
of Jane Austen's costumes coming and
going through parks and passages
into that sealed room
where who gets in
gets out
door locked
gate swinging on a broken hinge.

Ah, sweet mystery, the nature of
fact being fiction and fiction fact
she follows the chat, the storyline
whispers of human bartering –
and then and then and then and then –
she is sinking down into pillowy down
light as a feather – Jane's stories
tickle her fancy, blow her away.

Birney" (*Trio*), some lines are redistributed, and two words – "depositing / silver" – omitted in *Even Your Right Eye* – have been restored. In the same volume, line 7 of "Rust on an Anchor" – "that is to say" – has been revised to "a way to say." A definite article, "the" has been restored to the first line of "Sunday Morning Walk." In "Plankton nor Perch" (*The Sea Is Also a Garden*), the misprint "salmon" in the fifth line of the first stanza is corrected to "heron." Careful readers who know the texts well will discover a number of other alterations. However, Webb's revision of "The Colour of the Light" printed in the Thesen volume is followed here in *Peacock Blue*.

In this volume, the number of poems appearing in *Even Your Right Eye* is reduced from thirty-three to twenty-two in order to avoid repeating the eleven poems originally printed in *Trio,* in which section they can be found.

—JFH

Index of Titles and First Lines

Untitled poems are listed only by first line. End-of-line punctuation in each first line is retained as it appears in the original poem; ellipses indicate the continuing line of a prose poem.

In poems with numbered parts, only the first line of the first part is included.